WORLD OF Wonders
Developing Early Learners

Ready for Kindergarten

Mc Graw Hill Education

AUTHORS

Dr. Timothy Shanahan
University of Illinois at Chicago

Dr. Douglas Fisher
San Diego State University

Dr. Doris Walker-Dalhouse
Marquette University

Academic Advisors

Dr. Laura Justice
Ohio State University

Dr. Tracy Spinard
Arizona State University

Program Reviewers

Carol Barone-Martin
Pittsburgh Public Schools
Pittsburgh, PA

Shannon Cannon
Robla School District
Roseville, CA

Kimberly Russo
Pittsburgh Public Schools
Pittsburgh, PA

Dara Bleschman
JCP Downtown
New York City

Lisa Davis
Howard County Publish School System
Howard County, MD

Sarah Seymore
Visalia Unified School District
Visalia, CA

Cover and Title Page Art Credit: Aaron Zenz

Mister Rogers Growing & Changing is the copyright of The Fred Rogers Company and is used here with permission.

mhreadingwonders.com

Send all inquiries to:
McGraw-Hill Education
Two Penn Plaza
New York, NY 10121

ISBN: 978-0-07-678467-7
MHID: 0-07-678467-3

Printed in the United States of America.

1 2 3 4 5 6 7 8 9 RMN 21 20 19 18 17 16

Welcome to the World of Wonders

The McGraw-Hill *World of Wonders* program is a developmentally appropriate, research-based early learning curriculum. It is designed to prepare your youngest learners (3-, 4-, and 5-year-olds) for the academic and social demands of kindergarten. Our youngest learners are eager to explore the world of amazing wonders awaiting them and these instructional tools are carefully designed to assist you as you guide children on those explorations.

Table of Contents

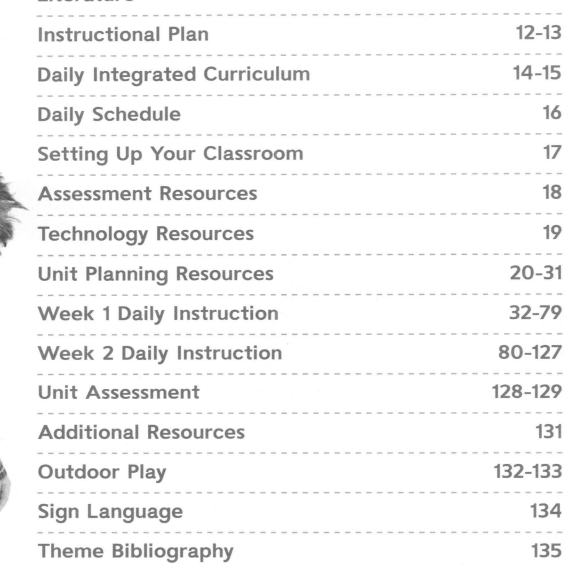

Ken Cavanagh/McGraw-Hill Education

Units

Unit 1
Who We Are
Children learn about the many things they can do and all the reasons they should feel good about themselves.

Unit 2
Making Friends
Children learn how to make friends, be a good friend, and about the fun things friends do together.

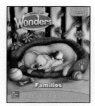

Unit 3
Families
Children learn what makes a family, what families do together, and how family members help each other.

Unit 4
Food
Children learn about different kinds of food, where food comes from, and how food changes when you cook it.

Unit 5
Our Neighborhood
Children learn about the many people and places in their neighborhood communities— from farms to cities.

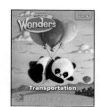

Unit 6
Transportation
Children learn about different ways to travel in the air, on the ground, and through the water, and how various vehicles are alike and different.

Unit 7
Animals
Children learn about taking care of pets, farm animals, animals in wild environments, and how animals grow and change.

Unit 8
Nature
Children learn about the wonders in nature, and how changes in the weather affect plants, animals, and people.

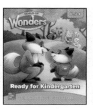

Unit 9
Ready for Kindergarten
Children review all that they've learned in the year and are assessed for kindergarten readiness.

Teacher's Choice Mini-Units
My Favorite Themes
Children learn about their favorite authors and illustrators, holidays, dinosaurs, and other favorite topics throughout the year.

Components

Teacher's Editions

Your *World of Wonders* Teacher's Editions provide weekly integrated lesson plans and professional resources, all divided into units organized around popular themes.

PreK Teacher's Editions

Literature

Classics and new stories, literary and informational text . . . you'll find a rich library of beloved selections.

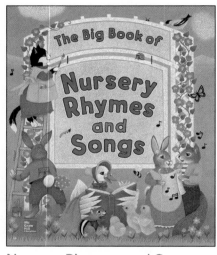

Nursery Rhymes and Songs

Big Books

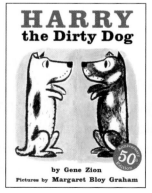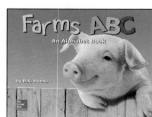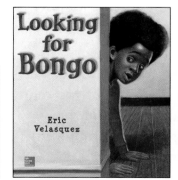

Trade Books

Read-Aloud Kit

Your students will enjoy classic tales, multicultural stories, nursery rhymes, and stories — the better to build background knowledge and overall literacy. Three Retelling Cards illustrate each Read-Aloud Anthology selection. As students talk about the key story events at the beginning, middle, and end, they are preparing to narrate and write.

Read-Aloud Anthology

Retelling Cards

Components
Additional Resources

The *World of Wonders* resources make lesson preparation easy, with social-emotional read-alouds, little books for early reading, reproducibles and activity pages for free-play, and Flip Charts for key content areas. Prefer to work online? You'll find it all on ConnectED. You'll also find professional development materials, key classroom routines, manipulatives and other materials to support your instruction.

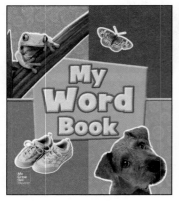

My Word Book

Social-Emotional

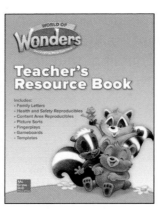

Teacher's Resource Book

Little Readers

Literacy and Language Flip Chart

Social-Emotional Flip Chart

Social Studies Flip Chart

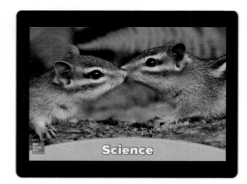

Science Flip Chart

Alphabet, Letter, Photo, Oral Language, and Concept Cards

Connecting to Kindergarten

In every unit, your students will build familiarity with the essential background knowledge and classroom routines that will make them successful in future years. They will:

- Build a strong foundation for literacy throughout the year

- Focus on math, science, social studies, and music in every unit

- Continue to develop their social-emotional skills

- Master key classroom routines designed for success in kindergarten

Unit 9, "Ready for Kindergarten," is the capstone of the year's learning.

PreK Teacher's Edition

Kindergarten Teacher's Edition

PreK Teacher's Edition

Kindergarten Teacher's Edition

Consistent features and support make transition to kindergarten easy.

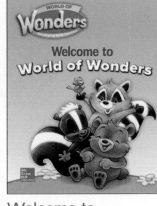

Welcome to World of Wonders

- Background research
- Built-in professional development
- Instructional routines
- Key resource links

 # Literature

	Unit 1 **Who We Are**	Unit 2 **Making Friends**	Unit 3 **Families**	Unit 4 **Food**	Unit 5 **Our Neighborhood**
WEEK 1	*Llama, Llama, Misses Mama* *Rosie Goes to Preschool*  Big Book	*Friends All Around* *Blue Chameleon*  Big Book	*Families* *Looking for Bongo*  Big Book	*Yummy! Good Food Makes Me Strong* *The Apple Pie That Papa Baked*  Big Book	*Say Hello!* *Whose Hat Is This?*  Big Book
WEEK 2	*If You're Happy* *Green Is a Chile Pepper* 	*Being Friends* *How Do Dinosaurs Play with Their Friends?* 	*All the World* *Big Box of Shapes* 	*Chew, Chew, Gulp!* *Plants Feed Me* 	*All Through My Town* *When Dinosaurs Came with Everything* 
WEEK 3	*Always, Sometimes, Never* *ABC I Like Me!* 	*Virgil & Owen* *ABC for You and Me* 	*Pecan Pie Baby* *Birthday Basket for Tia* 	*Feast for 10* *Bunny Cakes* 	*One Is a Drummer* *Round Is a Tortilla* 
WEEK 4	Teacher's Choice 	Teacher's Choice 	Teacher's Choice 	Teacher's Choice 	Teacher's Choice

Unit 6	Unit 7	Unit 8	Unit 9	Teacher's Choice
Transportation	**Animals**	**Nature**	**Ready for Kindergarten**	**My Favorite Themes**

The Bus For Us *Goodnight, Goodnight, Construction Site*  Big Book	*Farms ABC* *Duck, Duck, Goose* 	*Spring Is Here* *Leaves*  Big Book	*Dr. Seuss's ABC* 	**Eric Carle Author Study** *The Mixed-Up Chameleon*

Holidays

Thanks for Thanksgiving

Alphabeep: A Zipping, Zooming ABC *Clickety Clack* 	*What Puppies Do Best* *Gilbert Goldfish Wants a Pet* 	*Are Trees Alive?* *The Great Big Green* 	*I Know a Lot of Things* 	

Other Favorites

Tap the Magic Tree

If the Dinosaurs Came Back

Toy Boat *Row, Row, Row Your Boat* 	*Hello, Hello!* *Welcome Home Bear*  Big Book	*What Makes the Seasons* *Raindrop Plop!* 	

Flexible Teaching Options

World of Wonders offers opportunities for you to customize the instruction. In Week 4 of each unit, you can bring in your favorite theme-related books and activities. There is also My Favorite Themes — a collection of mini-units on popular themes (e.g. dinosaurs and holidays) for you to use throughout the year as you see fit.

Teacher's Choice 	Teacher's Choice 	Teacher's Choice

Instructional Plan
Developmentally Appropriate Lessons
Differentiated for All Learners

Developing Early Learners

World of Wonders provides differentiated pathways to address the needs of all early learners, whether serving a multi-age classroom or supporting the use of the same program over more than one year. A clear skills progression, background knowledge and familiarity with classroom routines place a strong focus on kindergarten readiness.

Starting Your Day/
Social-Emotional Development

- Daily Morning Message and Calendar activities reinforce literacy, math, science, and social studies skills

- Transitional activities provide review and built-in classroom management

- American Sign Language aids in quiet classroom management

- Meal Talk prompts for meaningful theme-related conversations

- Social-Emotional lessons by Mister Rogers to develop skills necessary for the demands of Kindergarten

- Weekly Social-Emotional books for enhanced learning

- Social-Emotional Flip Chart for on-the-spot teaching

(t) Fotos International/Archive Photos/Getty Images; (b) Ken Cavanagh/McGraw-Hill Education

Alphabet Time

- **Daily Circle Time** instruction addressing key literacy standards

- Daily differentiated Teacher Table support

- Clear instructional pathway for all learners (4-Year-Olds, 3-Year-Olds and Extra Support, Transitional K and Advanced Learners, English Learners, Adaptations for Children with Special Needs)

- Weekly Center activities (both free and guided play) with Purposeful Play Prompts, assessment links, support for building grammar and speaking skills, and a built-in Names and Pre-Writing Skills curriculum

Book Time

- **Daily Circle Time** activity followed by in-depth Teacher Table exploration

- Multiple books each week (new and classics) to provide options for students in the program more than one year

- Teacher's Choice week to incorporate favorite titles and activities

- Rich language and listening comprehension developed through a mix of fiction and nonfiction

- Cultural literacy through nursery rhymes and folk tales

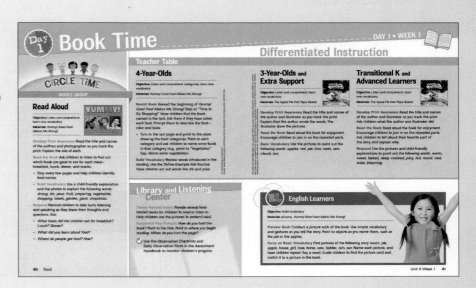

Daily Integrated Curriculum
Theme-based Learning

Science and Social Studies

- Daily whole- and small-group content lessons and hands-on activities tightly linked to unit theme

- Content-based read alouds to introduce concepts

- Photographic support (picture cards and online flip charts) to teach key concepts

- Journal prompts to express learning through writing

- Daily interactive centers (both free and guided play) and purposeful play prompts to support learning and exploration

Math

- Systematic and recursive scope and sequence to ensure mastery

- Daily in-depth lessons and support activities

- Access to additional instructional resources

- Manipulatives Kit for hands-on learning

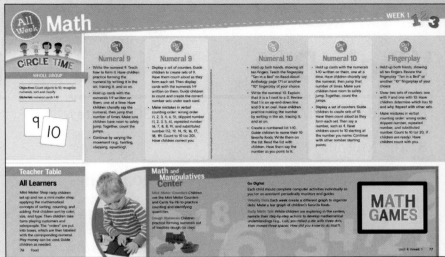

Music and Movement

- Weekly activities that meet music, dance, and physical development standards

- A wealth of songs (to download or stream) and additional music instruction through nursery rhymes

- Movement activities focusing on gross motor and fine motor skills, including indoor and outdoor play and morning movement routines

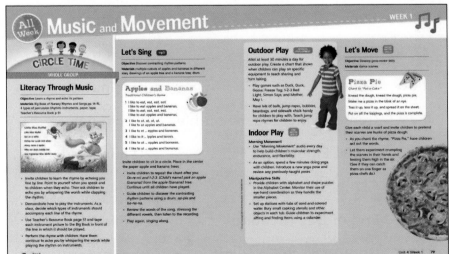

Daily Schedule

Whole Day

Time	Activity	Duration
8:00	Breakfast/Arrival	30 minutes
8:30	Morning Message	10 minutes
8:40	Alphabet Time	20 minutes
9:00	Center Time/Teacher Table	45 minutes
9:45	Book Time	20 minutes
10:05	Music and Movement	10 minutes
10:15	Snack/Meal Conversations	15 minutes
10:30	Outdoor Play	30 minutes
11:00	Science/Social Studies	20 minutes
11:20	Center Time/Teacher Table	40 minutes
12:00	Lunch	30 minutes
12:30	Rest Time	30 minutes
1:00	Math	20 minutes
1:20	Center Time/Teacher Table	30 minutes
1:50	Social-Emotional	20 minutes
2:10	Clean-Up	10 minutes
2:20	End of Day Meeting	20 minutes
2:40	Get Ready to Go Home	20 minutes
3:00	Dismissal	

Half Day

Time	Activity	Duration
8:00	Breakfast/Arrival	30 minutes
8:30	Morning Message	10 minutes
8:40	Alphabet Time	20 minutes
9:00	Center Time/Teacher Table	60 minutes
10:00	Book Time	20 minutes
10:20	Snack/Meal Conversations	15 minutes
10:35	Outdoor Play	30 minutes
11:05	Content Areas	20 minutes
11:25	Social-Emotional	20 minutes
11:45	Get Ready to Go Home	15 minutes
12:00	Dismissal	

Setting Up Your Classroom

Jobs Board Determine the list of classroom jobs. Each week assign one or two children to each job. Use their name cards on the Jobs Board (along with a picture) for easy reference. Add an icon for each job.

Calendar Display a monthly calendar. Use the calendar to discuss weather; the day's schedule; number recognition; and the concepts yesterday, today, and tomorrow.

Centers Set up these and other centers in special places around the classroom. At the beginning of each unit introduce the new center materials and help children establish learning goals. Explain that children should use art supplies carefully and be responsible for putting them away after they use them.

Alphabet	Library and Listening	Writing and Drawing
Dramatic Play	Computer	Math and Manipulatives
Science and Discovery	Social Studies	Art and Construction

Library Provide book and audio collections related to each unit's theme.

Teacher Table Use this table for small-group lessons, meeting the individual needs of all children.

Circle Time Area Provide a large space for children to gather where you can read books and teach whole-group lessons. Assign each child a space, using color mats or name cards.

Environmental Print Fill the room with environmental print including labels for classroom items, signs, charts, lists, and print found in your neighborhood.

Assessment
That Informs Instruction

Authentic Assessment

Performance Assessment

Observation occurs daily. Daily Observation Forms and Unit Checklists are provided to document each child's progress. Use these to form small groups for Teacher Table instruction.

Work Samples

Portfolios (print and electronic) are used to collect and evaluate each child's work. Retelling rubrics and forms are provided to record a child's progress and communicate to parents.

Developmental Red Flags

Observations of children's behavior and physical growth can help identify those children who need additional, formal evaluation for special services.

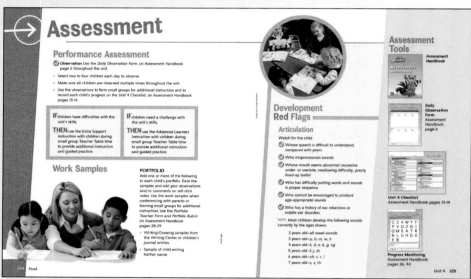

Formal Assessment

Use the Assessment Flip Book to periodically assess students' growth in language, math, and motor skills. Wordless books are also available to assess children's growing ability to use language in retelling stories or relating new information.

Assessment Flip Book

Technology

www.connected.mcgraw-hill.com

Digital Resources for You

 Plan
Customizable Lesson Plans

 Assess
Reports and Scoring

Teach
Classroom Presentation Tools
and Instructional Lessons

 School to Home
• Activities and Messages
• Family letters in nine languages

 Class Management
Student Grouping

 Professional Development
Model Lessons and
PD Videos

Additional Online Resources
• Instructional Flip Charts
• Teacher's Resource Book
• Assessment Handbook
• Welcome to PreK
• Alphabet, Music, Social-Emotional, and Content Area Songs

Digital Resources for Your Students

 Books
• e-Books
• Interactive Texts

Weekly Ideas for Families
• Activities and Games for Home
• Messages from the Teacher

 Words to Know
Handwriting Support

 Games
Interactive Games

READY FOR KINDERGARTEN

Focus Questions

ZouZou/Shutterstock.com

Unit 9 Planner

	WEEK 1	WEEK 2
Social-Emotional Development	**Mister Rogers:** New Experiences (Going New Places) **Social-Emotional Read Alouds:** Review **Flip Chart:** Review **Health and Safety:** Get a Check-up pp. 32–79	**Mister Rogers:** New Experiences (My First Day) **Social-Emotional Read Alouds:** Review **Flip Chart:** Review **Health and Safety:** Review pp. 80–127
Alphabet Time	**Phonological Awareness:** Review and Assess **Alphabet Recognition:** Review and Assess **Print Awareness:** Review and Assess **High-Frequency Word:** with **Little Reader:** *Will You Go With Me?* pp. 32–79	**Phonological Awareness:** Review and Assess **Alphabet Recognition:** Review and Assess **Print Awareness:** Review and Assess **High-Frequency Word:** for **Little Reader:** *Ready for Kindergarten* pp. 80–127
Book Time	*Dr. Seuss's ABC* **Read Aloud Anthology:** "The Tortoise and the Hare" **Emergent Writing** **Journal Prompts** pp. 32–79	**I Know a Lot of Things** **Read Aloud Anthology:** "The Turtle and the Flute" **Emergent Writing** **Journal Prompts** pp. 80–127
Social Studies/ Science	**Motion and Energy:** How Things Move **Growing Up:** What Our Bodies Need pp. 32–79	**Motion and Energy:** How Things Move **Growing Up:** Exercise Is Fun pp. 80–127
Math	Review and Assess pp. 32–79	Review and Assess pp. 80–127
Music and Movement	**Let's Sing:** "Mi cuerpo" (My Body) **Fine and Gross Motor Skills** **Outdoor Play** pp. 32–79	**Let's Sing:** "Gogo" **Fine and Gross Motor Skills** **Outdoor Play** pp. 80–127
Differentiated Instruction	*See instructional pathways for*: • 3-Year-Olds and Extra Support • Transitional K and Advanced Learners • English Learners • Adaptations for Children with Special Needs	*See instructional pathways for*: • 3-Year-Olds and Extra Support • Transitional K and Advanced Learners • English Learners • Adaptations for Children with Special Needs

Ready for Kindergarten

ASSESSMENT

Social-Emotional eBooks

Flip Chart

Theme and Transition Songs mp3

Alphabet Songs and Videos

Handwriting Videos and Resources

Little Reader eBooks

Photo and Alphabet Cards

Literacy Games

Big Book eBooks

Read Aloud Card Sequence Activity

Oral Language Cards

Vocabulary Glossary

Teacher's Choice Template

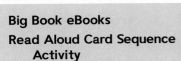

Science Flip Chart

Social Studies Flip Chart

Concept Cards

Content Area Games

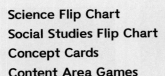

Math Games

My Favorite Songs mp3

Morning Movement songs

Teacher Edition and Lesson Planner

Assessment Resources

Student Portfolio

Theme Family Letters (9 languages)

State Correlations

Throughout this unit, you will complete each child's formal assessments (Assessment Flip Book) and performance assessment observations (Assessment Handbook), and finalize Student Portfolios.

- Circle Time instruction is provided, but Teacher Table time is reserved to give you ample opportunity to meet with each child individually.

- Be specific in terms of skills mastered and skills children are progressing toward mastery to inform each child's kindergarten teacher.

- You will also work with children to review and assess their growing social-emotional skill development in preparation for the demands of a kindergarten classroom.

Gather your Materials

Main Literature

WEEK 1

Dr. Seuss's ABC

WEEK 2

I Know a Lot of Things

Support Literature

The Big Book of Nursery Rhymes and Songs

Will You Go With Me?
Tell Me a Story
Tell Me About It

Social-Emotional Read Aloud

Ready for Kindergarten

Read-Aloud Anthology

Retelling Cards

Resource Books

My Word Book

Teacher's Resource Book *(includes Home-School Connections)*

Assessment Handbook

Assessment Flip Book

Flip Charts

Literacy and Language Flip Chart

Social Studies Flip Chart

Social-Emotional Flip Chart

Science Flip Chart

Manipulatives and More . . .

Contains:
- ✔ Counters
- ✔ Magnifying glass
- ✔ Instruments and more . . .

Manipulatives Kit

Oral Language, Alphabet, Letter, Photo, and Concept Cards

mp3

Audio Collections:
Music
Math
Social-Emotional

Meet the Standards

Go to mhreadingwonders.com for state-specific, Head Start, and other standards correlations.

(manipulatives) Ken Cavanagh/McGraw-Hill Education

Unit Centers

Purposeful Play Use the Purposeful Play Prompts in the daily lessons to engage children in conversation and knowledge-building while working in centers. See also the daily listening, speaking, and grammar skills focus.

Alphabet

Sound Matching Children play sound-matching games and connect letter-sound games.

Build a Name Children use magnetic letters, letter cards, clay, and art supplies to form their names in a special way.

Alphabet Puzzles Children engage with alphabet puzzles.

Library and Listening

Read and Listen Children read and listen to theme-related books, such as alphabet and "Welcome to Kindergarten" books.

e-Books Children engage with stories on tablets and other electronic hand-held devices.

Theme Books Children explore the week's theme books and little books, rereading them to partners.

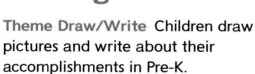

Writing and Drawing

Theme Draw/Write Children draw pictures and write about their accomplishments in Pre-K.

Pre-Writing Techniques Model and reinforce difficult strokes and letters while children freewrite.

Dramatic Play

Kindergarten Children role-play learning in a kindergarten classroom.

Doctor Doll Children pretend giving a checkup to a doll or helping an injured stuffed toy.

Retell and Act Children retell and act out scenes from favorite stories, using the pictures as aids.

Computer

Online Games Children play online literacy games—alphabet recognition, phonemic awareness, vocabulary sorts.

Computer Basics Review with children basic computer concepts, such as terms (*monitor, keyboard, mouse*) and various keys on the keyboard (*numbers vs letters, backspace, spacebar*). Help children use digital tools for writings and projects.

Math and Manipulatives

Counting Games Children engage in various games using dice and dominoes that require counting, adding, and subtracting.

Mini Motors Counters Children complete mini motors counting card activities to review skills.

Science and Discovery

Move It Children explore motion using toys with wheels, simple machines, ramps, water wheels, and other resources.

Using Energy Children explore how we get and use light, heat, electricity, and sound.

Social Studies

Doctor Children role-play a doctor using a doctor's kit, bandages, toy stethoscope, and other props.

Dentist Children pretend playing a dentist and dentist's patient.

Art and Construction

Body Art Children create fingerprint, thumbprint, and handprint designs and pictures.

Ready for Kindergarten Children illustrate the many ways they are ready for next year in school.

My Favorite Centers

List your own favorite centers for Unit 9 here.

_____

_____

_____

_____

_____

_____

_____

_____

Family and Community

Ideas for Busy Families

Teacher's Resource Book page 105

Home-School Connection

Theme-Related Books For Families

Send home a list of theme-related books for families to locate at their local library. Suggest they read several alphabet books each week. These books can include those used in the unit and those listed on the unit bibliography in the back of the Teacher's Edition. Remind families of the read aloud routine.

Step 1: Read the book the first time for enjoyment. Ask your child to share reactions to the book (e.g., interesting or surprising information).

Step 2: Reread the book on a subsequent day. Stop and discuss challenging words. Select 8-10 per book to focus on. Point to items in the pictures for your child to identify. Engage your child in discussions about the story plot or information learned from the book.

Step 3: Give the book to your child. Have him/her turn the pages and retell the story. Occasionally recast sentences with more sophisticated words. Encourage your child to draw or write about the book (e.g., their favorite part, what they learned).

Take-Home Games and Activities

Photo Ops Ask parents to send in photos of their children doing things they have learned throughout the year, such as writing their name. Use these photos as the basis for oral language and writing activities during Teacher Table or Center Time.

List of Accomplishments Ask families to create with their child a list of all the accomplishments he or she experienced throughout the year. Parents can add a note about what they've observed. Place the list in the child's portfolio.

Game Lending Library Set up a classroom game lending library. Have children "check out" favorite classroom games (e.g., literacy, math, puzzles) every week or every other week. Allow children to keep the game for several days to play with family members. This is an ideal way to engage families in fun at-home learning.

Ken Cavanagh/McGraw-Hill Education

Visit a Doctor's Office

Arrange for children to visit a local doctor's office to see what it looks like and what happens when you go for a checkup. Remind children that doctors and nurses are there to help them when they are injured or not feeling well.

Field Trips

Visit a School Nurse

Arrange for children to visit the school nurse to see where she is located and what happens when someone is sick. Take photos during the visit and use them as the basis for oral language and writing exercises. Discuss the tools the nurse uses and how to ask the nurse, or another adult, for help when injured or not feeling well.

Community Visitors

Invite a Doctor to Visit

Review parts of the body by inviting children to stand and play a game of Simon Says.

Explain to children that one way we take good care of our bodies is by getting a checkup with a doctor. Review what happens in a checkup using the "Doctor Doll" on Teacher's Resource Book page 106. Invite a doctor to visit the classroom to talk to children about taking care of their bodies.

Invite a Family Member

Invite any of children's family members (dad, mom, grandmother) who haven't been to the classroom yet to visit. Have children take the visitor around the classroom to share theme-related projects and writings. Prompt children to tell the visitor how they've grown and changed throughout the year. Family members can also read aloud a favorite theme-related book to the children to conclude their visit.

Theme Project

We're On Our Way

(tc, tr) BJI/Blue Jean Images/Getty Images

Tell children that throughout the unit they will be planning and preparing a graduation ceremony. Follow these steps (e.g., one step per week, or complete the entire project during Week 4).

Step 1   Remembering What We Did This Year

- Give each child all the pictures that were taken of him or her over the past year. Guide children to paste their pictures and design the pages. Collect their work. This will serve as their "diploma."

- Send letters home inviting family members to the graduation.

Step 2   Preparing for Graduation

- Select and practice a series of songs learned throughout the year.

- Help children make a banner for graduation. They can also make paper sashes to wear during the "ceremony."

Step 3   We're Big Kids Now!

- Let children sing the songs they prepared. Have a few children talk about the different things they've learned and what they liked most about Pre-K.

- Then call each one up to receive his or her special diploma.

My Favorite Theme Project

Record ideas below for additional **Ready for Kindergarten** theme projects you might do with children. Write the steps for each project and when you will complete the step during the unit.

My Project Idea #1: _____

_____

_____

Steps to Complete It _____

Step 1: _____

_____

Step 2: _____

_____

Step 3: _____

My Project Idea #2: _____

_____

_____

Steps to Complete It

Step 1: _____

_____

Step 2: _____

_____

Step 3: _____

_____

_____

Cards can be found on page 145 of the *Teacher's Resource Book*.

Week 1 Planner

ALL LEARNERS	DAY 1	DAY 2
Starting Your Day • Introduce Unit • Morning Message • Transitions that Teach • Sign Language • Meal Time Conversations	**Welcome to Unit 9** **Theme Song: "Teddy Bear"** **Introduce Theme Project** **Sign Language:** *yes, no* pp. 36-37	**Morning Message** **Meal Talk** **Transitions That Teach** pp. 44-45
Social-Emotional Development • Mister Rogers • Learning Through Literature • On-the-Spot Flip Chart	**Mister Rogers:** New Experiences (Going New Places) p. 37	**Mister Rogers:** New Experiences (Visit the Dentist) **Health and Safety:** Get a Checkup p. 45
Alphabet Time • Phonological Awareness • Alphabet Recognition • Print Awareness • High-Frequency Words • Emergent Reading • Purposeful Play Centers	**Alphabet Recognition:** Review ABCs **Phonological Awareness:** Syllables **Teacher Table:** Assess **Alphabet Center:** Sound-Matching Game pp. 38-39	**Alphabet Recognition:** Review ABCs **Handwriting:** Upper- and Lowercase Letters **Phonological Awareness:** Initial Sounds **Teacher Table:** Assess **Alphabet Center:** Sound-Matching Game pp. 46-47
Book Time • Book Handling • Vocabulary • Comprehension • Emergent Writing • Purposeful Play Centers	**Read Aloud:** *Dr. Seuss's ABC* **Teacher Table:** Reread and Build Vocabulary **Library Center:** Theme-Related Books  pp. 40-41	**Reread Aloud:** *Dr. Seuss's ABC* **Teacher Table:** Retelling **Journal Prompt** **Library Center:** Theme- Related Books pp. 48-49
Social Studies/Science • Integrated Content Areas • Purposeful Play Centers	**Motion and Energy:** How Things Move **Sing:** "Push and Pull" **Teacher Table:** Move It **Science Center:** Explore Motion pp. 42-43	**Motion and Energy:** How Things Move **Teacher Table:** Move It **Science Center:** Explore Motion **Focus on Speaking/Listening** pp. 50-51
Math • Systematic Instruction • Technology Differentiation • Purposeful Play Centers	**Review and Assess** **Computer Centers** pp. 76-77	**Review and Assess** **Computer Centers** pp. 76-77
Music and Movement • Music and Dance Standards • Gross Motor Skills • Fine Motor Skills • Outdoor Play	**Literacy Through Music:** "Teddy Bear" **Morning Movement** **Manipulative Skills** **Outdoor Play** pp. 78-79	**Let's Sing:** "Mi cuerpo" **Morning Movement** **Manipulative Skills** **Outdoor Play** pp. 78-79

DAY 3	DAY 4	DAY 5
Morning Message **Meal Talk** **Transitions That Teach** pp. 52-53	**Morning Message** **Meal Talk** **Transitions That Teach** pp. 60-61	**Morning Message** **Meal Talk** **Transitions That Teach** pp. 68-69

Social-Emotional
  Read Alouds: Review
Journal Prompt
 	
p. 53
	Social-Emotional
	  Read Alouds: Review
	Health and Fitness:
	  Get a Checkup
	
	p. 61
		Flip Chart: Review
		
		p. 69

Alphabet Recognition: Review ABCs **Handwriting:** Letters **Print Awareness:** Sentences **Teacher Table:** Assess **Alphabet Center:** Make Names **Focus on Grammar** pp. 54-55	**Alphabet Recognition:** Review ABCs **High-Frequency Word:** with **Teacher Table:** Assess **Alphabet Center:** Alphabet Puzzles **Focus on Grammar** pp. 62-63	**Alphabet Recognition:** Review ABCs **High-Frequency Word:** with **Teacher Table:** Assess **Alphabet Center:** Alphabet Fun pp. 70-71

Shared Writing:
  Alliterative Sentences
Teacher Table:
  Write About It
Writing/Drawing Center:
  Pre-Writing Techniques
pp. 56-57
	Read Aloud Anthology:
	  "The Tortoise and the Hare"
	Teacher Table: Revisit
	  Classic Tale
	Writing/Drawing Center:
	  Theme Write/Draw
	pp. 64-65
		Reread Aloud Anthology:
		  "The Tortoise and the Hare"
		Teacher Table: Revisit
		Journal Prompt
		Dramatic Play Center: Doctor
		Focus on Speaking pp. 72-73

Growing Up: What Our Bodies Need **Teacher Table:** Share and Read **Social Studies Center:** Doctor Doll pp. 58-59	**Growing Up:** What Our Bodies Need **Teacher Table:** Share and Read **Journal Prompt** **Social Studies Center:** Doctor Doll pp. 66-67	**Let's Pretend:** Let's Pretend **Art and Construction Center:** Body Art **Focus on Grammar** pp. 74-75
Review and Assess **Computer Centers** pp. 76-77	**Review and Assess** **Computer Centers** pp. 76-77	**Review and Assess** **Computer Centers** pp. 76-77
Let's Move: "Jack Be Nimble" **Morning Movement** **Manipulative Skills** **Outdoor Play** pp. 78-79	**Let's Sing:** "Teddy Bear" **Morning Movement** **Manipulative Skills** **Outdoor Play** pp. 78-79	**Morning Movement** **Manipulative Skills** **Outdoor Play** pp. 78-79

Ken Cavanagh/McGraw-Hill Education

Week 1 Planner

DIFFERENTIATED INSTRUCTION

	DAY 1	DAY 2
3-Year-Olds and Extra Support	**Alphabet Time:** Assess **Book Time:** *Dr. Seuss's ABC* Read and Build Basic Vocabulary **Science:** Oral Language pp. 39, 41, 43	**Alphabet Time:** Assess **Book Time:** *Dr. Seuss's ABC* Who? What? Where? **Science:** Let's Explore Together pp. 47, 49, 51
Transitional K and Advanced Learners	**Alphabet Time:** Assess **Book Time:** *Dr. Seuss's ABC* Read, Respond, and Extend Vocabulary **Science:** Oral Language pp. 39, 41, 43	**Alphabet Time:** Assess **Book Time:** *Dr. Seuss's ABC* Retell **Science:** Extend the Concept pp. 47, 49, 51
English Learners	**Alphabet Time:** Articulation Action Rhyme **Book Time:** Preview and Build Basic Vocabulary **Science:** Preteach Basic Words pp. 39, 41, 43	**Alphabet Time:** Review and Assess **Book Time:** Assess Oral Language **Science:** Develop Vocabulary pp. 47, 49, 51
Adaptations for Children with Special Needs	Modifications for Language Delays, Cognitive Delays, and Children on the Autism Spectrum p. 37	Modifications for Language Delays, Cognitive Delays, and Children on the Autism Spectrum p. 37

DIGITAL RESOURCES

Go Digital
- Teacher Resources
- Interactive Games and Activities
- Transitional K Small Group Planner

Digital Flip Charts
Theme and Transition Songs mp3
Morning Movement mp3
Alphabet Song Videos
Theme Book eBooks
Digital Teacher's Edition and Lesson Planner

Digital Flip Charts
Online Handwriting Videos and Resources
Digital Alphabet, Photo, and Concept Cards
Online Science Games

DAY 3

Alphabet Time: Assess
Book Time: Draw About It
Social Studies: Oral Language

pp. 55, 57, 59

Alphabet Time: Assess
Read: *Will You Go With Me?*
Book Time: Write About It
Social Studies: Oral Language

pp. 55, 57, 59

Alphabet Time: Review and Assess
Book Time: Assess Oral Language Write About It
Social Studies: Preteach Basic Words

pp. 55, 57, 59

Modifications for Physical Impairments, Vision Impairments, and Speech and Language Impairments

p. 53

DAY 4

Alphabet Time: Assess
Book Time: Build Basic Vocabulary
Social Studies: Let's Explore Together

pp. 63, 65, 67

Alphabet Time: Assess
Reread: *Will You Go With Me?*
Book Time: Vocabulary Boost
Social Studies: Extend the Concept

pp. 63, 65, 67

Alphabet Time: Review and Assess
Book Time: Assess Oral Language
Social Studies: Develop Vocabulary

pp. 63, 65, 67

Modifications for Physical Impairments, Vision Impairments, and Speech and Language Impairments

p. 53

DAY 5

Alphabet Assess
Book Time: Act It Out
Science/Social Studies: Review

pp. 71, 73, 75

Alphabet Time: Assess
Book Time: Retell
Science/Social Studies: Review

pp. 71, 73, 75

Alphabet Time: Review and Assess
Book Time: Develop Vocabulary Talk About It
Science/Social Studies: Review

pp. 71, 73, 75

Modifications for Behavior, Attention Deficit Disorder, and ADHD

p. 69

Digital Flip Charts
Social-Emotional eBooks
Little Reader eBooks
Digital Alphabet, Photo, Oral Language, and Concept Cards

Digital Flip Charts
Little Reader eBooks
Digital Retelling Cards
Online Social Studies Games

Digital Flip Charts
Online Math Games
Online Literacy Games
Digital Assessment Resources
Digital Student Portfolio

Day 1 Starting Our Day

Welcome to

Ready for Kindergarten

FOCUS QUESTIONS How have we grown and changed?
What are good health habits?

In this unit, children will learn about how they have grown, and what they need to do to stay healthy. Introduce the unit by doing the following:

- Display Literacy and Language Flip Chart page 46. Discuss what the children in the picture are doing, and how they are showing they are ready for kindergarten. Have children discuss their own experiences at school, and how they have grown and changed this year.

- Teach the Theme Song "Teddy Bear."

- Show children the new unit centers and set learning goals.

- Introduce the Theme Project on page 30, We're On Our Way.

UNIT 9

Unit 9 • Ready for Kindergarten   46

Ken Cavanagh/McGraw-Hill Education

SOCIAL-EMOTIONAL DEVELOPMENT

New Experiences

Going New Places

Grow and Learn with Mister Rogers

Objectives Use words to communicate thoughts and feelings; use play to work on feelings

Materials none

Tell children about a time when you were worried about going to a new place or having a new experience, such as riding a roller coaster or going to a relative's house. Then invite children to talk about a time when they felt scared about a new experience, such as

- going to a friend's house

- going to the doctor or dentist

- riding on a bus or airplane

Explain that one way to feel more comfortable in a new place is to take something comforting along with you, such as a toy, stuffed animal, or blanket. Encourage each child to tell you what he or she might take along to feel more comfortable in a new place.

→ *Transitions*

Theme Song Sing "Teddy Bear" between activities. See lyrics on Read Aloud Anthology page 170.

→ *Sign Language*

Teach the signs for *yes* and *no*. Use these for effective classroom management.

yes no

→ *Meal Talk*

What have we learned this year about eating healthy meals?

Adaptations for Children with Special Needs

Language Delays, Cognitive Delays, and Children on the Autism Spectrum

- These children might struggle learning weekly songs at the normal speed. Sing the song slowly when you introduce it, before using the audio file.

- Add Velcro dots to the ABC puzzles in the center to stabilize the small pieces. Place a hard Velcro dot on the puzzle base and a soft Velcro dot on the puzzle piece. This helps the pieces stay in place when the child is working or moving around with the puzzle.

(t) Fotos International/Archive Photos/Getty Images; (cr) Ken Cavanagh/McGraw-Hill Education

CiRCLE TiME

WHOLE GROUP

Alphabet Recognition

Objective Review Alphabet

Materials Letter Cards, tape, alphabet chart

Letter Review Secure letter cards for all 26 uppercase letters on the floor in random order to form a path. Have children hop the path as they say each letter name and sound.

Phonological Awareness

Objective Blend word parts

Materials Literacy and Language Flip Chart p. 48, Teacher's Resource Book p. 107

Word Parts Teach the poem "Jumping Beans." Hold up one finger for each number you say. Have children join in on a second reading.

Jumping Beans
One, two, three, four,
Beans come jumping through the door.
Five, six, seven, eight,
Jumping up onto my plate.

- Say a word from the poem in parts (syllable by syllable). Guide children to blend the parts to say the whole word.

- Continue by saying a word in parts (onset and rhyme) for children to blend.

- Conclude by saying a 2- or 3-letter word sound by sound for children to blend. Record your observations.

- Send home Teacher's Resource Book page 107 for more practice.

Teacher Table

4-Year-Olds

Objective Assess skills

Materials Assessment Handbook pp. 32–40

Assess Select several children to formally assess each day during Teacher Table time. Administer the tests individually. Record the results and your observations to determine each child's academic growth throughout the year and to inform the child's kindergarten teacher. Use these assessments from the Assessment Handbook.

- Names Assessment page 32

- Concepts of Print Assessment page 33

- Phonological Awareness Assessment pages 34–35

- Alphabet Assessment pages 36–37

- Comprehension Assessment pages 38–40

Alphabet Center

Sound-Matching Games Children match picture cards whose names begin with the same sound. Extend by having them match picture cards with letter cards.

Purposeful Play Prompts *What letter is this? What sound does it make? What words begin with that sound and letter?*

 Use the Observation Checklists and Daily Observation Form in the Assessment Handbook to monitor children's progress.

Differentiated Instruction

3-Year-Olds and Extra Support

Objective Assess skills

Materials Assessment Handbook pp. 32, 33, 36

Assess Select several children to formally assess each day during Teacher Table time. Administer the tests individually. Record the results and your observations to determine each child's academic growth throughout the year and to inform the child's next-year teacher. Use these assessments from the Assessment Handbook.

- Names Assessment page 32
- Concepts of Print Assessment page 33
- Alphabet Assessment page 36

Transitional K and Advanced Learners

Objective Assess skills

Materials Assessment Handbook pp. 32–40

Assess Select several children to formally assess each day during Teacher Table time. Administer the tests individually. Record the results and your observations to determine each child's academic growth throughout the year and to inform the child's kindergarten teacher. Use these assessments from the Assessment Handbook.

- Names Assessment page 32
- Concepts of Print Assessment page 33
- Phonological Awareness Assessment pages 34–35
- Alphabet Assessment pages 36–37
- Comprehension Assessment pages 38–40

Ken Cavanagh/McGraw-Hill Education

 English Learners

Objective Review alphabet

Materials Alphabet Song

Review Alphabet Sing the Alphabet Song with children. Then place a set of letter cards on the table.

- Have children take turns collecting the letter cards they recognize.
- Ask them to say the name (and sound, if appropriate) for each letter. Record your observations.

CiRCLE TiME
WHOLE GROUP

Read Aloud

Objective Listen and comprehend; learn new vocabulary

Materials *Dr. Seuss's ABC*

Develop Print Awareness Read the title and name of the author/illustrator as you track the print. Ask children to explain an author and illustrator's role in creating a book.

Read the Book Ask children to listen for the first letter in their name as you read the book.

- Before you read each page, point to the letter. Have children chorally say the letter name and sound. Ask them to name words that begin with the letter-sound.

- **Build Vocabulary** Use a child-friendly explanation and the pictures to explain the following words: *barber, camel, dozen, goggles, kettle, mumbling, ostrich, sipped, violin.*

Respond Remind children to take turns listening and speaking as they share their thoughts and questions. Ask:

- *What made the book fun to listen to?*

- *Which picture was your favorite? Why?*

- *How did you know which letter would come next?*

- *What order did the author put the letters in?*

Teacher Table

4-Year-Olds

Objective Discuss story structure

Materials *Dr. Seuss's ABC*, letter cards

Revisit Book Flip through *Dr. Seuss's ABC*. Stop periodically and ask: *What letter comes next?* Review that the book is in ABC order. Then spread a set of letter cards (A-Z) on the table. Start with uppercase letters. Have children work together to put the letters in order. Repeat with lowercase letters. Flip through the book again and have children match the upper- and lowercase letter cards to the correct book page.

Build Vocabulary Review the words introduced in the initial reading. Use the Define-Example-Ask Routine. Then have children gather a *dozen* counters and/or *mumble* something to a friend.

Library and Listening Center

Theme-Related Books Provide several alphabet books for children to read or listen to. Help children use the pictures to pretend-read.

Purposeful Play Prompts *How do you hold the book? Where are the words? The pictures? When do you turn the page?*

 Use the Observation Checklists and Daily Observation Form in the Assessment Handbook to monitor children's progress.

Differentiated Instruction

3-Year-Olds and Extra Support

Objective Listen and comprehend; learn new vocabulary

Materials *Dr. Seuss's ABC*

Develop Print Awareness Read the title and name of the author/illustrator as you track the print. Explain that the author wrote the words. He also drew the pictures.

Reread the Book Ask each child to name the first letter in his or her name. Chorally say the alphabet as you flip through the book until you get to the correct page. Read aloud the page. Ask the child if he or she knows any other words that begin with the same letter.

Basic Vocabulary Use the pictures to point out the following words: *alligator, bubbles, elephant, itchy, kite, six, umbrella.*

Transitional K and Advanced Learners

Objective Listen and comprehend; learn new vocabulary

Materials *Dr. Seuss's ABC*

Develop Print Awareness Read the title and name of the author/illustrator as you track the print. Ask children what an author and illustrator do in creating a book.

Read and Respond Read aloud the book for enjoyment. Encourage children to name the letter and sound as you turn each page. Ask children to tell about their favorite words or pictures from the book.

Boost Vocabulary Use the pictures and child-friendly explanations to point out the following words: *dozen, fluffy, goggles, itchy, lazy, mumbling, pink, quacking, sipped, awful, violin.*

 English Learners

Objective Build vocabulary

Materials pictures, *Dr. Seuss's ABC*

Preview Book Conduct a picture walk of the book. Prompt children to say each letter name before you read it. Point to objects as you name them, such as the *hat* or the *mice.*

Focus on Basic Vocabulary Find pictures of the following story nouns: *baby, egg, ear, jar, kite, leg, mice, six, ten.* Name each picture, and have children repeat. Say a word. Guide children to find the picture and match it to a picture in the book.

Day 1 Science

CiRCLE TiME

WHOLE GROUP

How Things Move

Objective Discuss motion

Materials Science Flip Chart p. 80

Share and Read Show children Flip Chart page 80, read the question, and discuss the photos. *What are the children doing? How are the objects moving?* Guide children to describe the motion of the objects pictured.

- Point to the picture of the children pulling on the toy. Ask: *What are these children doing?* (pulling) Explain that when you pull an object, you move it closer to you.

- Ask: *What is the opposite of pull?* (push) Explain that when you push an object, the object moves away from you. Ask: *Which picture shows something that is being pushed?*

Build Vocabulary Explain that *motion* is a change in an object's position. Write words and phrases that describe motion: *straight, zigzag, round and round, fast, slow.* Demonstrate each and prompt children to mimic you.

Journal Prompt Have children draw a picture of something that moves in the classroom or on the playground. Guide them to label the picture with a word or phrase to describe how it moves.

Motion

Teacher Table

4-Year-Olds

Objective Observe and experiment with motion

Materials toys with wheels, simple machine

How Does It Move?

Observe Show children an assortment of moving toys (e.g., vehicles) and simple machines. Demonstrate different movements and name them (e.g., *push, pull, straight line, zigzag*).

- Discuss the motion and position of each object. Emphasize the speed of the motion (e.g., *fast* or *slow*).

Explore Have children experiment with different ways to move objects and the range and speed of motion each has. Guide them to use academic language when discussing the movements. Introduce concepts of how things move— *mechanical, gravity, magnetism.*

Science and Discovery Center

Move It Have children experiment with motion using toys with wheels and simple machines. Set up ramps, water wheels, and other resources. Provide magnets, too.

Purposeful Play Prompts *What makes the toys move? What could you build or use so that it moved on its own? How can we make the car go faster? Further?*

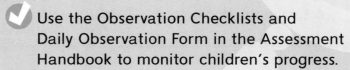 Use the Observation Checklists and Daily Observation Form in the Assessment Handbook to monitor children's progress.

Differentiated Instruction

3-Year-Olds and Extra Support

Objective Use vocabulary associated with motion

Materials toy vehicles, Science Flip Chart p. S13, audio

Oral Language Display the Flip Chart. Sing "Push and Pull" with children. Guide children to identify the toys pictured.

- Then provide some toys, such as a toy car or truck, for children to practice pushing and pulling. Prompt children to use the correct word (*push* or *pull*) to describe the action.

Transitional K and Advanced Learners

Objective Discuss motion

Materials Science Flip Chart p. 80

Oral Language Show children Flip Chart page 80. Ask questions about how each object moves. Have children mark the Flip Chart (e.g., circle the object).

- *Which water slide shows a straight line? Which shows a zigzag motion?*

- *Which rides go round and round? Which go fast? Slow?*

Ask children to write their name next to their favorite ride. Count the number of names to see which is the group's favorite.

 ## English Learners

Objective Learn vocabulary

Materials Concept Cards (170–174)

Preteach Basic Words Show children the motion-related Concept Cards. Point to each photo and name the motion (e.g., *pulling, sliding, spinning*). Have children repeat and demonstrate (where possible). Then say a movement. Guide children to match the photo cards to pictures in the unit's books or on the Science Flip Chart. Prompt them to repeat the photo name when they find a match.

☐ Welcome

Greet children and prompt them to return a greeting. Guide them to put away and organize their belongings. Remind children to put their name card on the attendance chart.

☐ Morning Message

- Gather children and sing the theme song "Teddy Bear."

- Remind children that they will be learning more about how we grow and change, and how we stay healthy.

> Sam plays with his friends.
> What do you do at school?

- Write a message to children. Read it aloud, tracking the print. Point out the week's high-frequency word *with*. Allow children time to respond to the question.

☐ Calendar and Daily Schedule

- Ask children what day it is. Write the sentence: Today is (<u>Tuesday</u>). Discuss what day yesterday was and what day tomorrow will be.

- Guide children to find the date on the calendar. Help a volunteer to write the date under the sentence. Have another volunteer read the date.

- Display and review today's schedule. Point out daily routines, the order of activities, and identify any special events.

- Choose one of the transition activities listed (or one of your own favorites) to move children into the next activity.

SOCIAL-EMOTIONAL DEVELOPMENT

New Experiences

Visit a Dentist

Grow and Learn
with Mister Rogers

Objective Try out different roles

Materials serving tray, dentist props, dolls or puppets with open mouths

Talk about a time when you went to the dentist to have your teeth cleaned. Explain that a dentist is a kind of doctor who helps people keep their teeth healthy.

- Set up a "dentist's office" for dolls or puppets. Place props on a tray.

- Show children what happens at a dentist's office. Put on a white shirt, mouth mask, goggles, etc. Use a tongue depressor to check inside a doll or puppet's mouth.

- Then review how to use a toothbrush.

- Place chairs next to the props and invite children to wait for their turn to visit the dentist.

Transitions

Literacy Say a sound (e.g., /s/). If the sound matches the first sound in a child's name, he or she can line up. Repeat until all children have lined up.

Math Have children line up by counting "as high as they can." Tap each child lightly as he or she says the next number in sequence before lining up.

Sign Language

Review the signs for *yes* and *no*, and continue to use previous signs.

Meal Talk

When have you visited a doctor? Why?

Health and Safety

Get a Checkup

Objective Learn the importance of a doctor's job

Materials stethoscope, tongue depressor, thermometer, scale, stuffed animals

Tell children that visiting the doctor for a checkup can be a new experience. Ask: *What do you know about visiting a doctor for a checkup?* Guide children to understand that routine checkups usually include weighing a patient; listening to his or her heartbeat; checking the patient's eyes, ears, and throat; and taking the person's temperature.

- Display the doctor's tools. Explain how each is used to check our health.

- Choose a stuffed animal and give it a checkup.

Alphabet Time

CiRCLE TiME

WHOLE GROUP

Alphabet Recognition

Objective Alphabet Assessment

Materials Letter Cards, tape, dry-erase boards, chart paper

Letter Review Secure letter cards for all 26 lowercase letters on the floor in random order to form a path. Have children hop the path as they say each letter name and sound.

Write Letters Give children dry-erase boards. Call out a letter. Ask children to write the letter. Then write the letter for children to self-correct. Continue with other letters. Record observations.

Phonological Awareness

Objective Review initial sounds

Materials Photo Cards

Initial Sounds Select 10-12 Photo Cards. Mix them.

- Display one card at a time. Ask children to name the animal, person, or object shown.

- Then ask them to name the first sound in the picture's name. Provide corrective feedback.

- Extend or reiterate the first sound to help children needing support.

Teacher Table

4-Year-Olds

Objective Assess skills

Materials Assessment Handbook pp. 32–40

Assess Select several children to formally assess each day during Teacher Table time. Administer the tests individually. Record the results and your observations to determine each child's academic growth throughout the year and to inform the child's kindergarten teacher. Use these assessments from the Assessment Handbook.

- Names Assessment page 32

- Concepts of Print Assessment page 33

- Phonological Awareness Assessment, pages 34-35

- Alphabet Assessment pages 36–37

- Comprehension Assessment pages 38–40

Alphabet Center

Sound-Matching Games Children match picture cards whose names begin with the same sound. Extend by having them match picture cards with letter cards.

Purposeful Play Prompts *What letter is this? What sound does it make? What words begin with that sound and letter?*

 Use the Observation Checklists and Daily Observation Form in the Assessment Handbook to monitor children's progress.

Differentiated Instruction

3-Year-Olds and Extra Support

Objective Assess skils

Materials Assessment Handbook pp. 32, 33, 36

Assess Select several children to formally assess each day during Teacher Table time. Administer the tests individually. Record the results and your observations to determine each child's academic growth throughout the year and to inform the child's next-year teacher. Use these assessments from the Assessment Handbook.

- Names Assessment page 32
- Concepts of Print Assessment page 33
- Alphabet Assessment page 36

Transitional K and Advanced Learners

Objective Assess skils

Materials Assessment Handbook pp. 32–40

Assess Select several children to formally assess each day during Teacher Table time. Administer the tests individually. Record the results and your observations to determine each child's academic growth throughout the year and to inform the child's kindergarten teacher. Use these assessments from the Assessment Handbook.

- Names Assessment page 32
- Concepts of Print Assessment page 33
- Phonological Awareness Assessment pages 34–35
- Alphabet Assessment pages 36–37
- Comprehension Assessment pages 38–40

Ken Cavanagh/McGraw-Hill Education

EL English Learners

Objective Review letter-sounds; build vocabulary

Materials Photo Cards

Review Letter-Sound Preview the Photo Cards from the Circle Time lesson. Display each card. Ask children to name the animal, person, or object pictured. Provide vocabulary, as needed. Say the picture name, emphasizing the initial sound (e.g., *sssssock, sock,* Sock *begins with the /s/ sound*).

Talk About It Have children talk about the pictures in English and their native language. Provide descriptive and action words, as needed.

Day 2 Book Time

CiRCLE TiME

WHOLE GROUP

Reread

Dr. Seuss's
ABc

Objective Focus on letter-sounds
Materials *Dr. Seuss's ABC*

Focus on Letter-Sounds Reread the book. Ask children to name each letter and sound before you read it. Observe which children readily answer and which remain quiet or answer in error. Record your observations. Ask:

- *What words on this page begin with [/s/]?*
- *What other words do you know for the [/s/] sound?*
- *What letter comes next in the alphabet?*

Journal Prompt Have children create a page for *Dr. Seuss's ABC*. Children can choose a letter in their name (e.g., first letter) or any other letter that interests them. Guide children to label each picture. Prompt them to write the first letter of each word. They can attempt to write the remaining letters, or you can complete the word for them.

Teacher Table

4-Year-Olds

Objective Focus on letter-sounds
Materials *Dr. Seuss's ABC,* pencil, paper

Focus on Letter-Sounds Say a sound. Have children work together to find the page in *Dr. Seuss's ABC* for the letter that matches the sound.

Write Letters Then ask children to write the letter. Observe their handwriting posture, pencil grip, and mastery of basic letter strokes.

Library and Listening Center

Theme-Related Books Provide several alphabet books for children to read or listen to. Help children use the pictures to pretend-read.

Focus on Speaking/Listening Guide children to express ideas and opinions about the books in complete sentences. Model by restating children's statements.

 Use the Observation Checklists and Daily Observation Form in the Assessment Handbook to monitor children's progress.

Differentiated Instruction

3-Year-Olds and Extra Support

Objective Focus on letter names

Materials *Dr. Seuss's ABC,* pencil, paper, name cards

Letter Names Give each child a name card. Have them find the page in the book that matches the first letter in their name.

Write Letter Have children write the letter. Observe their handwriting posture, pencil grip, and use of basic letter strokes. Record your observations.

Transitional K and Advanced Learners

Objective Focus on letter-sounds

Materials *Dr. Seuss's ABC,* pencil, paper

Focus on Letter-Sounds Say a sound. Have children work together to find the page in *Dr. Seuss's ABC* for the letter that matches the sound.

Write Letters Then ask children to write the letter. Observe their handwriting posture, pencil grip, and mastery of basic letter strokes.

Write Words Prompt children to write any words they know that begin with the same letter-sound. For simple short-vowel words, guide them to match a letter to each sound in the word. Model by stretching and isolating the sounds, then identifying the letter for that sound.

 **English Learners**

Objective Assess language

Materials *Tell Me a Story,* tape recorder

Assess Oral Language Individually, give each child a copy of *Tell Me a Story* (fiction). Have the child page through the book, examine the pictures, and tell the story using as many details as possible. Tape record the retelling. Then transcribe the recording and place in the child's portfolio as a record of their growing language skills.

CiRCLE TiME

WHOLE GROUP

Motion

Objective Discuss motion

Materials Science Flip Chart p. 80

How Things Move

Share and Read Review Flip Chart page 80. Ask: *What are the children doing? How are the objects moving?* Guide children to describe the motion of the objects pictures.

- Point out that these motions are mostly mechanical (i.e., machines). Display classroom machines that also have motion or bring in examples to share with children.

- Explain that there are other ways to move objects. For example, leaves fall from trees because of gravity (the pull from the earth). Drop an object to demonstrate. In addition, certain metal objects move when a magnet is near them. Briefly demonstrate and review with children their experiments with magnetism earlier in the year.

- **Build Vocabulary** Remind children that *motion* is a change in an object's position. Review words and phrases that describe motion: *straight, zigzag, round and round, fast, slow*. Demonstrate a motion and prompt children to describe it using one of the words.

Motion

Teacher Table

4-Year-Olds

Objective Observe and experiment with motion

Materials toys with wheels

How Does It Move?

Observe Continue to show children an assortment of moving toys (e.g., vehicles) and simple machines. Demonstrate different movements and name them (e.g., *push, pull, straight line, zigzag*). Discuss the motion and position of each object. Emphasize the speed of the motion (e.g., *fast* or *slow*).

Explore Have children experiment with different ways to move objects and the range and speed of motion each has. Guide them to use academic language when discussing the movements. Review concepts of how things move—*mechanical, gravity, magnetism.*

Science and Discovery Center

Move It Have children experiment with motion using toys with wheels and simple machines. Set up ramps, water wheels, and other resources. Add magnets, too.

Focus on Listening/Speaking Guide children to use conversational rules when discussing concepts with you, such as listening without interrupting, turn-taking, and using appropriate intonation. Stop and model, as needed.

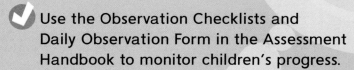 Use the Observation Checklists and Daily Observation Form in the Assessment Handbook to monitor children's progress.

Differentiated Instruction

3-Year-Olds and Extra Support

Objective Explore motion

Materials toys with wheels

Let's Explore Together Show children an assortment of moving toys, such as vehicles. Demonstrate different movements and name them (e.g., *push, pull, straight line, zigzag*). Have children mimic and say the motion word(s). Then discuss the position of each object and the speed of the motion (e.g., *fast* or *slow*). Name a movement, speed, or position for children to model using the toy.

Ken Karp/McGraw-Hill Education

Transitional K and Advanced Learners

Objective Explore motion in the environment

Materials paper, pencils, journals

Extend the Concept Take children to the school playground. Have them look around for playground equipment that moves, such as swings and seesaws. Ask children to draw pictures in their journals of the playground equipment that moves and write a caption for each one.

When you return to the class, have children share their pictures and read their captions. Prompt them to explain how the equipment moves using words and phrases such as *straight line, zigzag, up and down, back and forth, round and round, fast,* and *slow.*

 English Learners

Objective Develop concept vocabulary

Materials Concept Cards, online games

Develop Vocabulary Use the Concept Cards and online science games to develop children's theme-related vocabulary. Have children play the games independently and with partners. The visual and audio supports reinforce and build word knowledge. Use the photo to play matching and sorting games. Identify each picture name and have children repeat before, during, and after play.

SCIENCE GAMES

Starting Our Day

☐ Welcome

Greet children by singing the "Hello Song" or another favorite greeting song. Guide children to put away and organize their belongings. Prompt children to put their name card on the attendance chart.

☐ Morning Message

- Gather children and sing the theme song "Teddy Bear."

- Remind children that they will be learning more about how we grow and change, and how we stay healthy.

- Write a message to children. Read it aloud, tracking the print. Point out the week's high-frequency word *with*. Allow children time to respond to the question.

> I went to the store with my friend.
>
> Where have you gone with a friend?

☐ Calendar and Daily Schedule

- Ask children what day it is. Write the sentence: Today is (Wednesday). Discuss what day yesterday was and what day tomorrow will be.

- Guide children to record the weather using a symbol, such as a sun or a cloud. Ask: *What was the weather like yesterday?*

- Display and review today's schedule. Point out daily routines, the order of activities, and identify any special events.

- Choose one of the transition activities listed (or one of your own favorites) to move children into the next activity.

SOCIAL-EMOTIONAL DEVELOPMENT

Review

Objective Listen to a read aloud

Materials Social-Emotional Read Alouds

Read and Reflect Display all eight Social-Emotional Read Alouds. Guide children to revisit the covers. Track the print as you read each title.

- Tell children that they have learned a lot about how to act in school and be a good friend, and that they can feel proud of their accomplishments.

- Guide children to tell one way the learned to be a good friend.

- Explain to children that next year in school they will make even more new friends. Have children role-play how to introduce themselves to someone new. Provide a model, if needed.

Journal Prompt Have children draw a picture showing them being a good friend. Ask them to write or dictate a sentence for their picture.

(tl) Art'nLera/Shutterstock.com

Transitions

Literacy Have children clap the syllables in their name as they line up.

Math Place number cards 2–10 on the floor in sequence. Have each child line up next to the number that matches the number of letters in his or her first name.

Sign Language

Review the signs for *yes* and *no*, and continue to use previous signs.

Meal Talk

How can you help your friends?

Adaptations for Children with Special Needs

Physical, Vision, and Speech and Language Impairments

- For music activities, provide simple props to help children focus on the actions (e.g., scarves). If children have difficulty grasping musical instruments, add a soft elastic band to the handle.

- Use a black marker and ruler to simplify cutting activities. Draw straight lines between or around pictures on reproducibles. Straight lines are easier for children to cut out. In sorting activities, place the pictures or objects on high-contrast yellow or black sheets of laminated paper.

CiRCLE TiME

WHOLE GROUP

Alphabet Recognition

Objective Review Alphabet

Materials Letter Cards, paper, pencils, crayons, finger paint

Letter-Sound Review Hide (easily visible) letter cards around the room. Have children find them and name each letter and its sound. Discuss each letter's attributes (e.g., curves, straight lines, name).

Write Letters Have children sort letter cards by attribute (e.g., letters formed with all straight lines). Once the sets are formed, have children write the letters from each set on separate sheets of paper. Children can use pencils, crayons, or finger paint.

Print Awareness

Objective Recognize sentences

Materials chart paper

Sentences Write the sentence *We can read.*

We can read.

- Say: *This sentence has three words. Watch as I point to each word and count it. Now it's your turn. Count with me: 1, 2, 3.*

- Then point out that the first word in a sentence begins with a capital, or uppercase, letter. Circle the capital *W*. Also point out the period at the end of the sentence. Repeat with other sentences.

Teacher Table

4-Year-Olds

Objective Assess skills

Materials Assessment Handbook pp. 32–40

Assess Select several children to formally assess each day during Teacher Table time. Administer the tests individually. Record the results and your observations to determine each child's academic growth throughout the year and to inform the child's kindergarten teacher. Use these assessments from the Assessment Handbook.

- Names Assessment page 32
- Concepts of Print Assessment page 33
- Phonological Awareness Assessment pages 34-35
- Alphabet Assessment pages 36–37
- Comprehension Assessment pages 38–40

Alphabet Center

Build a Name Children use magnetic letters, letter cards, clay, art supplies, and other resources to form their names.

Focus on Grammar Model how to create longer sentences by combining children's ideas.

✔ Use the Observation Checklists and Daily Observation Form in the Assessment Handbook to monitor children's progress.

Differentiated Instruction

3-Year-Olds and Extra Support

Objective Assess skills

Materials Assessment Handbook pp. 32, 33, 36

Assess Select several children to formally assess each day during Teacher Table time. Administer the tests individually. Record the results and your observations to determine each child's academic growth throughout the year and to inform the child's next-year teacher. Use these assessments from the Assessment Handbook.

- Names Assessment page 32
- Concepts of Print Assessment page 33
- Alphabet Assessment, page 36

Transitional K and Advanced Learners

Objective Add sounds, read connected text

Materials Photo Cards, *Will You Go With Me?*

Add Sounds Display Photo Cards 26-30. Tell children you will say a word part. You want them to add /f/ to the beginning to make a word, then find the matching photo. Model with /an/ to make *fan*.

Read *Will You Go With Me?* Read the title. Have children repeat. Model sounding out *will*.

- Have children point to each word as they chorally read it with you. Stop and provide corrective feedback (e.g., model sounding out a word). Read the book twice.

- **Check Comprehension** Ask: *What can you do now that you couldn't do when you started school?* Prompt children to answer in complete sentences.

EL English Learners

Objective Build theme-related vocabulary

Materials Oral Language Cards (138–144)

Oral Language Display the Oral Language Cards. Name each picture and have children repeat the name. Then say a movement. Guide children to perform the action, then find the matching picture.

Talk About It Place the Oral Language Cards facedown. In turn, have children select a card. Help children identify the item and describe the action (e.g., *The boy is sleeping.*). Provide language as needed.

English-Spanish run/correr, jump/saltar, clap/aplaudir, swim/nadar, sleep/dormir, sit/sentar

Ken Cavanagh/McGraw-Hill Education

Book Time

CiRCLE TiME

WHOLE GROUP

Shared Writing

Objective Write an alliterative sentence

Materials chart paper, marker, *Dr. Seuss's ABC*

Write an Alliterative Sentence Flip through the book. Read a few sample pages. Emphasize the first sound of the words for each target letter. Ask: *Which words begin with the same sound?*

- Write one of the sentences on the chart, such as *Vera Violet Vinn is very very very awful on her violin.* Prompt children to circle all the letter V's.

- Then select another letter-sound. Brainstorm with children words that begin with that letter-sound.

- Use these words to create an alliterative sentence with children. Create several sentences, one per letter-sound.

Sounds Alike

Sam sat on his sandwich.

Teacher Table

4-Year-Olds

Objective Write an alliterative sentence

Materials *Dr. Seuss's ABC,* paper, pencils, assortment of alphabet books

Write About It Have children create an alliterative sentence for the first letter in their name. Children can flip through *Dr. Seuss's ABC* and other alphabet books for ideas.

- Help children create a list of possible words to include in their sentence.

- Share the pen by having children write the focus letter, then write the remaining letters.

- Have children practice and share their sentences with the class.

Writing and Drawing Center

Pre-Writing Technique Model line strokes that children struggle with. Observe and provide corrective feedback as children write. Additional handwriting resources are available online.

Purposeful Play Prompts Ask children: *How do you hold your pencil? What sound does the word begin with? What letter do you write for that sound?*

 Use the Observation Checklists and Daily Observation Form in the Assessment Handbook to monitor children's progress.

Differentiated Instruction

3-Year-Olds and Extra Support

Objective Write (draw/create) an alliterative phrase

Materials *Dr. Seuss's ABC*

Draw About It Have children draw a picture of themselves. Ask them to write their name under their picture. Then guide children to think of a word that describes them—a word that begins with the same letter-sound as their name. Offer possible word choices. Write the word children choose in front of their name to create an alliterative phrase (e.g., *Silly Sam*).

Transitional K and Advanced Learners

Objective Write an alliterative sentence

Materials *Dr. Seuss's ABC,* paper, pencils, assortment of alphabet books

Write About It Have children create an alliterative sentence for the first letter in their name. Children can flip through *Dr. Seuss's ABC* and other alphabet books for ideas.

- Help children create a list of possible words to include in their sentence.

- Share the pen with children as needed. Guide them to think about each sound in simple short-vowel words they write and attach a letter to each sound.

- Have children practice and share their sentences with the class.

 English Learners

Objective Assess language

Materials *Tell Me a Story,* tape recorder

Assess Oral Language Individually, give each child a copy of *Tell Me a Story* (fiction). Have the child page through the book, examine the pictures, and tell the story using as many details as possible. Tape record the retelling. Then transcribe the recording and place in the child's portfolio as a record of their growing language skills.

CiRCLE TiME
WHOLE GROUP

What Our Body Needs

Objective Understand what our body needs

Materials Social Studies Flip Chart p. 49

Share and Read Tell a volunteer that you are going to pretend to tickle him or her. Ask the class: *If I really tickled someone, what might happen?* Tell children that they can make predictions by using what they already know to figure out what might happen next.

- Display the Flip Chart. Have children describe each photo. Using the photos, give a child-friendly explanation to point out the words *rest* and *healthy*.

- Read the question. Explain to children what our body needs each day to be at its best (e.g., rest, healthful food, water, and exercise).

- Discuss with children what happens when our body doesn't get what it needs daily, such as feeling bad when we don't get enough sleep. Invite children to name things they can do to feel good and be at their best.

Body Needs

Teacher Table

4-Year-Olds

Objective List ways to stay healthy

Materials paper, crayons, chart paper

Draw It Give each child a sheet of construction paper. Help children fold the paper into three equal sections. Discuss with children what they do to stay healthy. Make a list on chart paper.

- Have children number the sections on their paper 1, 2, 3.

- Ask them to draw in each section one way they stay healthy (e.g., get enough sleep, exercise, eat healthful foods, visit a doctor).

Social Studies Center

Doctor Provide props, such as a plastic doctor's kit with stethoscope, for children to pretend playing doctor.

Purposeful Play Prompts Work with children to use specific health-related words as they share what they're doing in the center. *What do you do with a stethoscope? How does a doctor help you?*

✔ Use the Observation Checklists and Daily Observation Form in the Assessment Handbook to monitor children's progress.

Differentiated Instruction

3-Year-Olds and Extra Support

Objective List ways to stay healthy
Materials paper, crayons, chart paper

Oral Language Give each child a sheet of construction paper. Help the children fold the paper in half. Discuss with children what they do to stay healthy.

- Help children number the sections on their paper 1, 2. Ask them to draw in each section one way they stay healthy (e.g., get enough sleep, exercise, eat healthful foods, visit a doctor).

- Ask questions about children's drawing to prompt them to use new health-related words.

Transitional K and Advanced Learners

Objective List ways to stay healthy
Materials paper, crayons, chart paper

Draw It Give each child a sheet of construction paper. Help the children fold the paper into three equal sections. Discuss with children what they do to stay healthy. Make a list on chart paper.

- Have children number the sections on their paper 1, 2, 3. Ask them to draw in each section one way they stay healthy (e.g., get enough sleep, exercise, eat healthful foods, visit a doctor).

- Then have children write a sentence to describe each picture. Prompt children to write letters and words they know. Model and guide them as they write (e.g., *What's the first sound in* sleep? *What letter do we write for the /s/ sound?*).

 **English Learners**

Objective Learn vocabulary
Materials Concept Cards (165-169)

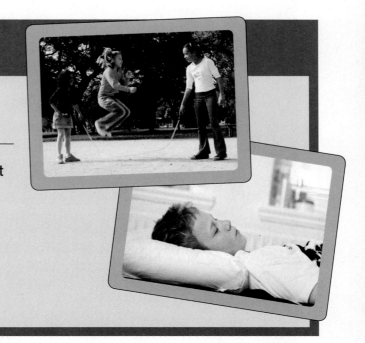

Preteach Basic Words Show children the health-related Concept Cards. Point to each and name it (e.g., *eating*). Pantomime an action. Have children find the matching photo and name it. Provide sentence frames for children to talk about the pictures (e.g., *He/She is _____.*).

Starting Our Day

☐ Welcome

Greet children and guide them to put away and organize their belongings. Prompt children to put their name card on the attendance chart.

☐ Morning Message

- Gather children and sing the theme song "Teddy Bear."

- Remind children that they will be learning more about how we grow and change, and how we stay healthy.

- Write a message to children. Read it aloud, tracking the print. Point out any uppercase letters and end punctuation. Allow children time to respond to the question.

> We had a fun year!
> What did we learn this year?

☐ Calendar and Daily Schedule

- Ask children what day it is. Write the sentence: Today is (<u>Thursday</u>). Discuss what day yesterday was and what day tomorrow will be.

- Sing the "Days of the Week" song. Guide children to find the letter or alphabet card that matches the first letter of the day's name (e.g., T). Count with children the number of letters in the day's name.

- Display and review today's schedule. Point out daily routines, the order of activities, and identify any special events.

- Choose one of the transition activities listed (or one of your own favorites) to move children into the next activity.

SOCIAL-EMOTIONAL DEVELOPMENT

Review

Objective Listen to a read aloud

Materials Social-Emotional Read Alouds

Reread and Reflect
Distribute the books, one book per small group of children. Prompt children to talk with their friends about the stories and what they remember.

- Throughout the week, take pictures of children making good choices, being good friends, solving problems with words, and showing respect. Share and discuss the photos with children. Invite them to reflect on how they can make good choices each day.

- As children collaborate, encourage them to identify their preferences when making choices and listen to others before speaking.

(tl) Art'nLera/Shutterstock.com

Transitions

Music/Movement Sing "Did You Clean Up" to the tune of "Are You Sleeping, Are You Sleeping, Brother John?"

Did you clean up?
Did you clean up?
Please make sure.
Please make sure.
Everything is picked up.
Everything is picked up.
Please. Thank you!
Please. Thank you!

Sign Language

Review the signs for *yes* and *no*, and continue to use previous signs.

Meal Talk

What are you most excited to do or learn in kindergarten?

 Health and Safety

Get a Checkup

Objective Review the importance of a doctor's job

Materials stethoscope, tongue depressor, thermometer, scale, stuffed animals

Remind children that visiting the doctor for a checkup can be a new experience, but it is important to keep yourself healthy. Review the doctor's tools.

- Explain that a stethoscope lets the doctor listen to a patient's heartbeat.

- A tongue depressor helps a doctor to see a patient's throat.

- A thermometer checks a patient's temperature.

- Have children color, cut out, and glue the clothing and tools to make the doctor doll on Teacher's Resource Book page 106.

Alphabet Time

CIRCLE TIME

WHOLE GROUP

Alphabet Recognition

Objectives Review alphabet

Materials Letter Cards, picture cards

Letter-Sound Review Hold up a letter card. Have children say the letter name and perform the action (e.g., sing the letter song).

Compare Letter-Sounds Display Photo Cards (create a set of 6-8).

• Say each picture name, stressing the initial sound.

• Guide children to find the letter card (from a corresponding set of 6-8) that matches the first sound in the picture word.

High-Frequency Word

Objectives Read and write high-frequency words

Materials chart paper

Teach *with* Use the Read-Spell-Write Routine to teach *with*.

• **Read** Write the word *with*. Point to it. Say: *This is the word* with. *What is the word?*

• **Spell** Point to each letter and say its name. Repeat and have children join in. Say: With *is spelled* w-i-t-h.

• **Write** Have children write the word (or trace it) as they say each letter name.

Teacher Table

4-Year-Olds

Objectives Assess skills

Materials Assessment Handbook pp. 32-40

Assess Select several children to formally assess each day during Teacher Table time. Administer the tests individually. Record the results and your observations to determine each child's academic growth throughout the year and to inform the child's kindergarten teacher. Use these assessments from the Assessment Handbook.

• Names Assessment page 32

• Concepts of Print Assessment page 33

• Phonological Awareness Assessment pages 34-35

• Alphabet Assessment pages 36-37

• Comprehension Assessment pages 38-40

Alphabet Center

Alphabet Puzzles Stock the center with alphabet puzzles. Sing the Alphabet Song with children, pointing to each letter in the puzzle. Prompt children to point to and name letters they know.

Focus on Grammar Model how to create longer sentences by combining children's ideas (e.g., *What letters are in your name? Yes, the letters* a *and* m *are both in your name.*).

 Use the Observation Checklists and Daily Observation Form in the Assessment Handbook to monitor children's progress.

Differentiated Instruction

3-Year-Olds and Extra Support

Objectives Assess skills

Materials Assessment Handbook pp. 32, 33, 36

Assess Select several children to formally assess each day during Teacher Table time. Administer the tests individually. Record the results and your observations to determine each child's academic growth throughout the year and to inform the child's next-year teacher. Use these assessments from the Assessment Handbook.

- Names Assessment page 32
- Concepts of Print Assessment page 33
- Alphabet Assessment page 36

Transitional K and Advanced Learners

Objectives Read connected text

Materials letter and word cards, *Will You Go With Me?*

Letter-Sound Review Use letter cards to review letter-sounds. Then display word cards for children to blend: *can, am, on, hot, it, big, egg, red, up, bug.*

Reread *Will You Go With Me?* Reread the book with children.

- Have children point to each word as they chorally read it. Stop and provide corrective feedback. Then have children read it to a partner.

- **Retell and Write** Have children retell what they learned to a partner, using the photos. Then have them draw and write about something they want to do or learn in kindergarten. Provide a sentence frame for support: *I can ____.*

 ## English Learners

Objective Build vocabulary

Materials Concept Cards (165-169)

Review Basic Words Show children the Concept Cards. Point to each picture and name it (e.g., *sleeping*). Pantomime an action. Have children find the matching picture and name it. Provide sentence frames for children to talk about the pictures (e.g., *He/She is ____.*).

Talk About It Give each child the card pile. Prompt children to say: *The boy/girl is ____* as they flip through the pictures.

CiRCLE TiME

WHOLE GROUP

Classic Tale

Objective Listen and comprehend; learn new vocabulary

Materials Retelling Cards; Read-Aloud Anthology p. 94

The Tortoise and the Hare
Display the first Retelling Card and have children discuss the illustration. Connect *hare* to *rabbit/bunny* and *tortoise* to *turtle* to help children. Then read the story and have them listen to find out what happens when the tortoise and hare race. Ask: *Who do you think will win the race? Why?* Display the other cards as prompted.

Respond Have children discuss the story and what they think the hare learned about racing a tortoise.

Teacher Table

4-Year-Olds

Objective Learn new vocabulary
Materials Retelling Cards

Revisit Tale Display the Retelling Cards for "The Tortoise and the Hare" and guide children to put them in order. Have children describe what is happening in each scene. Ask: *Which animals do you see? What are they doing? Who is winning the race?*

Build Vocabulary Explain the words *boast* and *confident* using the Define-Example-Ask Routine.

- **Define** *Boast* means "to brag or speak very highly about yourself."

- **Example** *My sister likes to boast that she is a great swimmer.*

- **Ask** *What have you heard someone boast about?*

Writing and Drawing Center

Theme Write/Draw Children write about the many things they accomplished this year in school—things they are proud of.

Purposeful Play Prompts Ask children: *What are you drawing or writing about?* Write labels and sentences they dictate for their drawings to review that print conveys meaning.

 Use the Observation Checklists and Daily Observation Form in the Assessment Handbook to monitor children's progress.

Differentiated Instruction

3-Year-Olds and Extra Support

Objective Learn new vocabulary

Materials Retelling Cards

Revisit Tale Display the Retelling Cards for "The Tortoise and the Hare" and guide children to put them in order.

Basic Vocabulary Use the illustrated scenes to build basic vocabulary. Prompt children to point to various characters, actions, and things as you name them. Use descriptive words when naming them, such as "the slow tortoise" or the "fast hare." Then name an item or character pictured and have children find and describe it (e.g., *Find the tortoise. Tell me about him.*).

Transitional K and Advanced Learners

Objective Learn new vocabulary

Materials Retelling Cards

Revisit Tale Display the Retelling Cards for "The Tortoise and the Hare" and guide children to put them in order. Have children describe what is happening in each scene. Ask: *Where are the tortoise and hare? Who is winning the race?*

Vocabulary Boost Explain the words *boast, confident, amazed, slowpoke, leaped,* and *snooze,* using the Define-Example-Ask Routine.

- **Define** *Confident* means "sure" or "certain."

- **Example** *I feel confident that I can write my name.*

- **Ask** *What do you feel confident about?* Provide sentence frames using the words for children to complete (e.g., *I feel confident about _____.*).

English Learners

Objective Build vocabulary

Materials pictures, Retelling Cards, "The Tortoise and the Hare"

Preview Story Display the three Retelling Cards, one at a time. Use simple vocabulary and gestures as you tell the story. Use 1-2 sentences per card. Point to characters and objects as you name them, such as the tortoise, hare, forest, and nap.

Focus on Basic Vocabulary Find pictures of the following story words: *tortoise, hare, forest, nap, race.* Name each picture, and have children repeat. Play I Spy. Say a word (e.g., *I spy a _____.*). Guide children to find the picture and say the picture name as they pick it up.

Ken Cavanagh/McGraw-Hill Education

Day 4 Social Studies

CiRCLE TiME

WHOLE GROUP

What Our Bodies Need

Objective Understand what our body needs

Materials Social Studies Flip Chart p. 49, audio

Share and Read Display the Flip Chart and review what our bodies need to stay healthy (e.g., sleep, eat healthful foods, exercise, drink water, visit a doctor).

- Review the words *rest* and *healthy* and what happens when our body doesn't get what it needs daily, such as feeling bad when we don't get enough sleep.

- Perform some simple exercises children can do daily to stay healthy, such as yoga poses using the "Morning Movement" audio.

- Then take children outside to play games involving running, such as freeze tag. Give children water after exercising, explain its importance, and allow children to discuss how exercising makes them feel.

Journal Prompt *What do you need to stay healthy?*

Body Needs

Teacher Table

4-Year-Olds

Objective List ways to stay healthy

Materials paper, crayons, chart paper

Draw It Continue to work with children on their "staying healthy" pictures.

- Make sure each child has a sheet of construction paper. Help children fold the paper into three equal sections.

- Discuss with children what they do to stay healthy. Guide children to number the sections on their paper 1, 2, 3.

- Ask them to draw in each section one way they stay healthy (e.g., get enough sleep, exercise, eat healthful foods, visit a doctor).

Social Studies Center

Doctor Provide props, such as a plastic doctor's kit with stethoscope, for children to pretend playing doctor.

Focus on Listening/Speaking Guide children to use conversational rules when discussing concepts with you, such as listening without interrupting and turn-taking.

 Use the Observation Checklists and Daily Observation Form in the Assessment Handbook to monitor children's progress.

Differentiated Instruction

3-Year-Olds and Extra Support

Objective List ways to stay healthy

Materials paper, crayons, chart paper

Oral Language Continue to explore with children ways to stay healthy.

- Give each child a sheet of construction paper. Help the children fold the paper in half.

- Discuss with children what they do to stay healthy. Help children number the sections on their paper 1, 2. Ask them to draw in each section one way they stay healthy (e.g., get enough sleep, exercise, eat healthful foods, visit a doctor).

- Ask questions about children's drawing to prompt them to use new health-related words.

Transitional K and Advanced Learners

Objective List ways to stay healthy

Materials paper, crayons, chart paper

Draw It Continue to explore with children ways to stay healthy. Give each child a sheet of construction paper. Help the children fold the paper into three equal sections. Discuss with children what they do to stay healthy. Make a list on chart paper.

- Have children number the sections on their paper 1, 2, 3. Ask them to draw in each section one way they stay healthy (e.g., get enough sleep, exercise, eat healthful foods, visit a doctor).

- Then have children write a sentence to describe each picture. Prompt children to write letters and words they know. Model and guide them as they write (e.g., *What's the first sound in* sleep*? What letter do we write for the /s/ sound?*).

 **English Learners**

Objective Develop concept vocabulary

Materials Concept Cards, online games

Develop Vocabulary Use the Concept Cards and online social studies games to develop children's theme-related vocabulary. Have children play the games independently and with partners. The visual and audio supports reinforce and build word knowledge. Use the cards to play matching and sorting games. Identify each picture name and have children repeat before, during, and after play.

SOCIAL STUDIES GAMES

Starting Our Day

☐ Welcome

Greet children and guide them to make eye contact with you as they return a greeting. Remind children to put away and organize their belongings, and prompt them to put their name card on the attendance chart.

☐ Morning Message

- Gather children and sing the theme song "Teddy Bear."

- Remind children that they will be learning more about how we grow and change, and how we stay healthy.

- Write a message to children. Read it aloud, tracking the print. Have children point out any letters and words they know. Contrast letters with numbers when looking at the calendar. Allow children time to respond to the question.

> I like to read.
> What do you like to do?

☐ Calendar and Daily Schedule

- Ask children what day it is. Write the sentence: Today is (Friday). Discuss what day yesterday was and what day tomorrow will be.

- Review the days of the week using the "Days of the Week" song. Clap the syllables of each day's name as you say it.

- Display and review today's schedule. Point out daily routines, the order of activities, and identify any special events.

- Choose one of the transition activities listed (or one of your own favorites) to move children into the next activity.

SOCIAL-EMOTIONAL DEVELOPMENT

Making Good Choices

Objective Discuss making good choices at school

Materials Social-Emotional Flip Chart

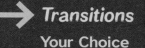

Making Good Choices

Social-Emotional

I Make Good Choices Display the Social-Emotional Flip Chart. Flip through the pages and stop on any concepts children need to review.

- Examine the picture with children and ask the questions provided.

- Complete any projects (writing, creating pictures, or enacting scenes) related to the Flip Chart page you didn't have time to address earlier in the year.

- Have children re-enact the page, modeling how to act or respond in the situation pictured.

WEEKLY TIP Encourage children to show respect for friends by complimenting them.

(tl) Art'nLera/Shutterstock.com

Transitions
Your Choice

_____

_____

_____

_____

Sign Language
Review the signs for *yes* and *no*, and continue to use previous signs.

Meal Talk
What is your favorite thing we did this year together?

Adaptations for Children with Special Needs

Behavior Problems, Attention Deficit Disorder, and ADHD

- State what is not acceptable behavior, such as pushing or falling on someone, before doing a physical activity. Offer frequent praise and positive reinforcement.

- Use masking or colored duct tape as visual supports for the environment. Place a strip on the floor where children line up. Use tape arrows to show proper movement pathways and tape lines to define clear borders between centers and activity areas.

Day 5 Alphabet Time

CiRCLE TiME

WHOLE GROUP

Alphabet Recognition

Objectives Read a theme-related book

Materials *My Word Book* (Book 10), crayons

Read *Stay Fit!* Help children tear off and fold the book.

- Read the book to children. Use the directions at the bottom of each page to guide the instruction and discussion.

- Send home the book for children to share with their families.

High-Frequency Word

Objectives Read and write high-frequency words

Materials chart paper

Review *with* Use the Read-Spell-Write Routine to review *with*.

- **Read** Write the word *with*. Point to it. Say: *This is the word* with. *What is the word?*

- **Spell** Point to each letter and say its name. Repeat and have children join in. Say: With *is spelled* w-i-t-h.

- **Write** Have children write the word (or trace it) as they say each letter name. Have children create oral sentences using the word *with*. Write their sentences. Share the pen by having them write *with*.

Teacher Table

4-Year-Olds

Objectives Assess skills

Materials Assessment Handbook pp. 32-40

Assess Select several children to formally assess each day during Teacher Table time. Administer the tests individually. Record the results and your observations to determine each child's academic growth throughout the year and to inform the child's kindergarten teacher. Use these assessments from the Assessment Handbook.

- Names Assessment page 32

- Concepts of Print Assessment page 33

- Phonological Awareness Assessment pages 34-35

- Alphabet Assessment pages 36-37

- Comprehension Assessment pages 38-40

Alphabet Center

Alphabet Fun Use the online literacy games to develop children's skills. Have children play the games independently and with partners. The visual and audio supports reinforce and build letter knowledge and phonemic awareness.

ALPHABET GAMES

 Use the Observation Checklists and Daily Observation Form in the Assessment Handbook to monitor children's progress.

Differentiated Instruction

3-Year-Olds and Extra Support

Objectives Assess skills

Materials Assessment Handbook pp. 32, 33, 36

Assess Select several children to formally assess each day during Teacher Table time. Administer the tests individually. Record the results and your observations to determine each child's academic growth throughout the year and to inform the child's next-year teacher. Use these assessments from the Assessment Handbook.

- Names Assessment page 32
- Concepts of Print Assessment page 33
- Alphabet Assessment page 36

Transitional K and Advanced Learners

Objectives Write words with short vowels

Materials word cards, letter cards

Write Words with Short Vowels Display word cards for children to blend: *can, am, on, hot, it, big, egg, red, bug, up.*

- Then guide children to write each word. Model segmenting the word sound-by-sound and attaching a letter to each sound.
- For children needing support, give them the letter cards needed to form the word. Guide them to place the letter cards in order as you say each sound in the word.

 English Learners

Objective Build theme-related vocabulary

Materials Oral Language Cards (138-144)

Oral Language Display the movement Oral Language Cards. Review each picture and have children repeat. Perform (mimic) the action, then say: *Now you try.*

Talk About It Pretend-play with children in the Dramatic Play Center using objects that move (e.g., toy cars). Name the items that children pick up and prompt them to name or describe how each moves. Reinforce the actions on the Oral Language Cards.

CiRCLE TiME

WHOLE GROUP • READ ALOUD

Classic Tale

Objective Listen and comprehend; begin to retell story events

Materials Retelling Cards; Read-Aloud Anthology p. 94

Reread and Model Retelling
Reread the story. Use the Retelling Cards to model a retelling. Then guide children in identifying the setting; telling who the characters are; and describing what happens first, next, and so on. Use a sequence graphic organizer to record these events as children state them.

Journal Prompt Have children draw a picture from the story and write a retelling. Have them dictate sentences to describe their picture. Review that the sentence begins with an uppercase, or capital, letter, and ends with the correct punctuation mark.

Teacher Table

4-Year-Olds

Objective Listen and retell; practice new vocabulary

Materials Retelling Cards; Read-Aloud Anthology p. 94

Guided Retell Place the Retelling Cards on the table. Have children take turns putting them in the proper sequence (beginning, middle, end). Then have children retell the story using the pictures. Listen in and direct children to provide missing details. Prompt them using the questions on the back of each card.

Dramatic Play Center

Doctor Provide props, such as a plastic doctor's kit with stethoscope, for children to pretend playing doctor.

Focus on Speaking Focus children on speaking clearly and in complete sentences with proper subject-verb agreement. Model, as needed.

 Use the Observation Checklists and Daily Observation Form in the Assessment Handbook to monitor children's progress.

Differentiated Instruction

3-Year-Olds and Extra Support

Objective Listen and retell; practice new vocabulary

Materials Retelling Cards; props, fingerplay puppets, Teacher's Resource Book p. 109

Act It Out Provide props or fingerplay puppets for children to act out the story. See Teacher's Resource Book page 109. Assign children parts. Allow children to retell the story multiple times, switching the child who plays the parts of the tortoise and the hare. Display the Retelling Cards so children can use them to aid in retelling.

Transitional K and Advanced Learners

Objective Listen and retell; practice new vocabulary

Materials Retelling Cards

Retell Place the Retelling Cards on the table. Have children work together to put them in the proper sequence (beginning, middle, end). Then have children retell the story to a partner. They can use the Retelling Cards as reference. Circulate and listen in on the retellings. Prompt children to predict what they think will happen the next time hare is challenged to a race.

 English Learners

Objective Listen and retell; practice new vocabulary

Materials Retelling Cards; pictures

Develop Vocabulary Review the pictures for the story nouns: *tortoise, hare, forest, nap, race.* Name each picture, and have children repeat. Say a word. Guide children to find the picture and say the picture name as they pick it up. Then have children name a picture for their classmates to find.

Talk About It Display the Retelling Cards, one at a time. Ask children to name items in each picture. Then act out the scene depicted as you state a sentence to summarize what you are doing (e.g., *The tortoise napped.*). Have children repeat the actions while saying the sentence.

Day 5 Hands-On

CiRCLE TiME

WHOLE GROUP

Let's Pretend

Objective Develop the ability to play creatively and learn more about our bodies

Materials cloth to make bandages

What's Under the Bandage? Explain to children that grown-ups sometimes put bandages on hurt body parts to help the body parts stay clean, not move, and get better. Tell children that bandages don't change the skin and body parts under them—they just help the body parts get better.

- Wrap a strip of cloth around your arm like a bandage and let a child unwind it and take it off to see that your arm is still underneath.

- Ask children if they want to have a part of their body, such as an elbow or a knee, wrapped up by you. Wrap it and then let them unwrap their own bandage.

- Invite children to wrap their own leg, foot, arm, or other body part. They can wear their bandage for a while and pretend with it.

Teacher Table

4-Year-Olds

Objective Pretend play a doctor

Materials doll, bandages, play doctor's kit

Doll Doctor Remind children that one way to take care of ourselves is to visit a doctor and dentist. Explain that doctors take care of our general health and dentists focus on the care of our teeth.

- Display the dolls, bandages, doctor's kit, and any other health-related props.

- Have children perform a checkup on their doll. If the doll is injured they can wrap the wound in a bandage. This is also a good time to review medicine safety.

- Monitor children's use of health-related language and provide new or more specific vocabulary, as needed.

Art and Construction Center

Body Art Children create paintings using finger-, thumb-, and handprints.

Focus on Grammar Work with children to use "my" or "mine" to indicate their work, and "his" or "her" to identify the work of others. Model as needed.

 Use the Observation Checklists and Daily Observation Form in the Assessment Handbook to monitor children's progress.

Differentiated Instruction

3-Year-Olds and Extra Support

Objective Pretend play a doctor

Materials doll, bandages, play doctor's kit

Doll Doctor Remind children that one way to take care of ourselves is to visit a doctor and dentist. Explain that doctors take care of our general health and dentists focus on the care of our teeth.

- Display the dolls, bandages, doctor's kit, and any other health-related props.

- Have children perform a checkup on their doll. If the doll is injured they can wrap the wound in a bandage. This is also a good time to review medicine safety.

- Monitor children's use of health-related language and provide new or more specific vocabulary, as needed.

Transitional K and Advanced Learners

Objective Pretend play a doctor

Materials doll, bandages, play doctor's kit

Doll Doctor Remind children that one way to take care of ourselves is to visit a doctor and dentist. Explain that doctors take care of our general health and dentists focus on the care of our teeth.

- Display the dolls, bandages, doctor's kit, and any other health-related props.

- Have children perform a checkup on their doll. If the doll is injured they can wrap the wound in a bandage. This is also a good time to review medicine safety.

- Monitor children's use of health-related language and provide new or more specific vocabulary, as needed.

Ken Cavanagh/McGraw-Hill Education

 English Learners

Objective Develop vocabulary

Materials health tool props or photos

Develop Vocabulary Display the health tool props and photos. Add a label to each photo. Double label the photos where possible (e.g., medicine/medicina). Use the photos to build and reinforce vocabulary. Provide sentence frames for children to use the new terms in conversation (e.g., *This is a _____.*). Have children select a photo they feel comfortable with and discuss it with a friend using English and their native language.

CiRCLE TiME

WHOLE GROUP

Objectives Review and assess

Materials Assessment Handbook

Shapes Review

- Display a set of shape manipulatives (e.g., the shape buttons) and pictures of shapes. Have children match a manipulative to each shape. Then have children sort the shapes. Ask them to explain their sorting rule.

- Place a set of shape blocks in a bag. Have children grab a shape from the bag and describe it to the class. Confirm identity by revealing the shape. Then place a pile of shapes on the table, multiples of each shape. Call out a shape name for children to find. Have them hold up their shape.

Counting Review

- Guide children to count as high as they can as you march around the room. Take note of where children "trail off." Review counting to 30.

- Display a set of counters. Ask: *How many do I have?* Have children chorally count, then name the amount. Repeat with amounts from 0-30.

- Distribute the dominoes cards on Teacher's Resource Book pages 113-114. Have children work together to count and match the amounts.

(l) Nadezhda1906/Shutterstock.com; (lc) McGraw-Hill Education; (rc, r) Ken Cavanagh/McGraw-Hill Education

Teacher Table

All Learners

Assessment Select several children to assess each day during Teacher Table time. Administer the tests individually. Record the results and your observations to determine each child's academic growth throughout the year and to inform the child's kindergarten teacher. Use these assessments from the Assessment Handbook: Counting, Numbers, Shapes, Patterns, Colors, Sorting.

Math and Manipulatives Center

Math Games Children engage with games requiring counting, include games with dice and dominoes.

Mini Motor Counters Children use the counters and cards to review and practice Pre-K math skills.

Numerals Review

- Place the numeral cards on the table in random order. Have children work together to order them.

- Display a numeral card (0-10). Have children create a matching set of counters.

Counting Review

- Display 3 sets of counters—two with the equal number. Ask children to find the sets that match.

- Place a small set of counters in your hand. Briefly open your hand. Ask: *How many do I have?* Then close you hand. Record children's responses. Open your hand and chorally count with children to confirm.

Addition and Subtraction Review

- Use counters and simple word problems to guide children to add to 5. Extend based on children's abilities.

- Use counters and simple word problems to guide children to subtract from 5. Extend based on children's abilities.

Go Digital

Each child should complete computer activities individually as you (or an assistant) periodically monitor and guide.

Weekly Data Each week create a different graph to organize data. You might also wish to take an existing graph and display the information in a new way (e.g., change a T-chart into a bar graph). Ask questions about the graph's content and connect the information to mathematical concepts.

Daily Math Talk While children are exploring in the centers, use narrating, revoicing, and asking open-ended questions to develop mathematical understandings and problem-solving skills. Discuss with children the strategies they are using.

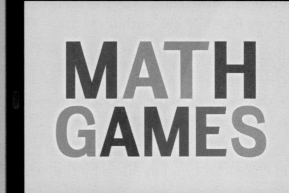

CiRCLE TiME

WHOLE GROUP

Literacy Through Music

Objective Practice left-to-right tracking

Materials Big Book of Nursery Rhymes pp. 16-17, Teacher's Resource Book p. 115, tapping pieces

Teddy Bear

Teddy bear, teddy bear,
Turn around.

Teddy bear, teddy bear,
Show your shoe.

Teddy bear, teddy bear,
Touch the ground.

Teddy bear, teddy bear,
That will do.

16   17

A tapping page is an excellent way to help children work on left-to-right tracking.

- Play the recording and have children show the movements of the song. (For the complete song lyrics, see Read-Aloud Anthology page 170.)

- Display the Big Book and invite children to join you singing the song as you point to each word.

- Place the tapping page, Teacher's Resource Book page 115, on a table so all can see.

- Introduce the small manipulative used to tap the page. Place this tapping piece by the arrow.

- Demonstrate tapping through each line of the page while singing the rhyme. Invite children to sing with you as they tap with their fingers.

Let's Sing

Objective Move to show rhythmic patterns

Materials audio, rhythm instruments

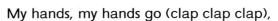

Mi cuerpo (My Body)

Spanish Folk Song

English Version by McGraw-Hill

My body makes music,
It's easy, you will see.

My body makes music,
It's easy, you will see.

My hands, my hands go (clap clap clap),

My feet, my feet go (stamp stamp stamp),

My mouth, my mouth goes "La la la,"

My body does the "Cha cha cha."

Play the recording and invite children to move to the music.

- Demonstrate the repeating rhythm pattern using movement and sound: hands (clap clap clap), feet (stamp stamp stamp), sing ("La la la"), and wiggle ("Cha cha cha").

- Review the words of the song, then invite children to sing along with the recording and move to show the repeating rhythm pattern. (Optional: Teach the Spanish version, available on the audio.)

- Play again and invite children to sing and play rhythm instruments on the rhythmic patterns.

Outdoor Play PHYSICAL DEVELOPMENT

Allot at least 30 minutes a day for outdoor play. Create a chart that shows when children can play on specific equipment to teach sharing and turn taking.

- Play games such as Duck, Duck, Goose; Freeze Tag; 1-2-3 Red Light; Simon Says; and Mother, May I.

- Have lots of balls, jump ropes, beanbags, bubbles, and sidewalk chalk handy for children to play with. Teach jump rope rhymes for children to enjoy.

Indoor Play FINE MOTOR SKILLS

Morning Movement
- Use "Morning Movement" audio every day to help build children's muscular strength, endurance, and flexibility.

- As an option, spend a few minutes doing yoga with children. Introduce a new yoga pose and review any previously-taught poses.

Motor Assessment
- Formally assess children's motor skills using the Motor Assessments in the Assessment Flip Book.

- Use the following assessments: hopping, walking a straight line, throwing a ball, catching a ball, kicking a ball, holding a pencil correctly, drawing lines, writing first name, and cutting a straight line.

Ken Cavanagh/McGraw-Hill Education

Let's Move GROSS MOTOR SKILLS

Objective Develop gross-motor skills

Materials blocks, audio

Jack Be Nimble

Traditional Nursery Rhyme
Music by Randy DeLelles

(Sung) Jack, be nimble, Jack, be quick,
Jack, jump over the candlestick.
(Spoken) Oh, no, no, no!
That's not the thing to do.
Don't jump over the candlestick,
You might just burn your shoe!

Give each child a block to use as a "candlestick." Have children listen to the recording and help them notice that it has two sections. Have them:

- Echo-speak the rhyme with you.

- Place their candlestick on the floor and practice jumping over it.

- Sing the rhyme while jumping over the candlestick.

Week 2 Planner

ALL LEARNERS	DAY 1	DAY 2
Starting Your Day • Introduce Unit • Morning Message • Transitions that Teach • Sign Language • Meal Time Conversations	**Welcome to Unit 9** **Theme Song:** "Teddy Bear" **Introduce Theme Project** **Sign Language:** *please, wait* pp. 36-37	**Morning Message** **Meal Talk** **Transitions That Teach** pp. 44-45
Social-Emotional Development • Mister Rogers • Learning Through Literature • On-the-Spot Flip Chart	**Mister Rogers:** New Experiences (My First Day) p. 37	**Mister Rogers:** New Experiences (Musical Performances) **Health and Safety:** Review p. 45
Alphabet Time • Phonological Awareness • Alphabet Recognition • Print Awareness • High-Frequency Words • Emergent Reading • Purposeful Play Centers	**Alphabet Recognition:** Review ABCs **Phonological Awareness:** Syllables **Teacher Table:** Assess **Alphabet Center:** Sound-Matching Game pp. 38-39	**Alphabet Recognition:** Review ABCs **Handwriting:** Upper- and Lowercase Letters **Phonological Awareness:** Initial Sounds **Teacher Table:** Assess **Alphabet Center:** Sound-Matching Game pp. 46-47
Book Time • Book Handling • Vocabulary • Comprehension • Emergent Writing • Purposeful Play Centers	**Read Aloud:** *I Know a Lot of Things* **Teacher Table:** Reread and Build Vocabulary **Library Center:** Theme-Related Books 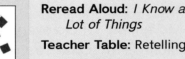 pp. 40-41	**Reread Aloud:** *I Know a Lot of Things* **Teacher Table:** Retelling **Journal Prompt** **Library Center:** Theme-Related Books pp. 48-49
Social Studies/Science • Integrated Content Areas • Purposeful Play Centers	**Motion and Energy:** Energy and Electricity **Teacher Table:** Move It **Science Center:** Explore Energy pp. 42-43	**Motion and Energy:** Energy and Electricity **Teacher Table:** Move It **Science Center:** Explore Motion **Focus on Speaking/Listening** pp. 50-51
Math • Systematic Instruction • Technology Differentiation • Purposeful Play Centers	**Review and Assess** **Computer Centers** pp. 76-77	**Review and Assess** **Computer Centers** pp. 76-77
Music and Movement • Music and Dance Standards • Gross Motor Skills • Fine Motor Skills • Outdoor Play	**Literacy Through Music:** "Teddy Bear" **Morning Movement** **Manipulative Skills** **Outdoor Play** pp. 78-79	**Let's Sing:** "Gogo" **Morning Movement** **Manipulative Skills** **Outdoor Play** pp. 78-79

DAY 3	DAY 4	DAY 5
Morning Message **Meal Talk** **Transitions That Teach** pp. 52-53	**Morning Message** **Meal Talk** **Transitions That Teach** pp. 60-61	**Morning Message** **Meal Talk** **Transitions That Teach** pp. 68-69
Social-Emotional Read Alouds: Review **Journal Prompt** p. 53	**Social-Emotional Read Alouds:** Review **Health and Fitness:** Review p. 61	**Flip Chart:** Review p. 69
Alphabet Recognition: Review ABCs **Handwriting:** Letters **Print Awareness:** Sentences **Teacher Table:** Assess **Alphabet Center:** Make Names **Focus on Grammar** pp. 54-55	**Alphabet Recognition:** Review ABCs **High-Frequency Word:** with **Teacher Table:** Assess **Alphabet Center:** Alphabet Puzzles **Focus on Grammar** pp. 62-63	**Alphabet Recognition:** Review ABCs **High-Frequency Word:** with **Alphabet Center:** Assess **Alphabet Center:** Alphabet Fun pp. 70-71
Shared Writing: Alliterative Sentences **Teacher Table:** Write About It **Writing/Drawing Center:** Pre-Writing Techniques pp. 56-57	**Read Aloud Anthology:** "The Turtle and the Flute" **Teacher Table:** Revisit Classic Tale **Writing/Drawing Center:** Theme Write/Draw pp. 64-65	**Read Aloud Anthology:** "The Turtle and the Flute" **Teacher Table:** Revisit Classic Tale **Journal Prompt** **Dramatic Play Center:** Doctor **Focus on Speaking** pp. 72-73
Growing Up: Exercise Is Fun **Teacher Table:** Share and Read **Social Studies Center:** Doctor Doll pp. 58-59	**Growing Up:** Exercise Is Fun **Teacher Table:** Share and Read **Journal Prompt** **Social Studies Center:** Doctor Doll pp. 66-67	**Let's Pretend:** Let's Pretend **Art and Construction Center:** Body Art **Focus on Grammar** pp. 74-75
Review and Assess **Computer Centers** pp. 76-77	**Review and Assess** **Computer Centers** pp. 76-77	**Review and Assess** **Computer Centers** pp. 76-77
Let's Move: "Minuet II" **Morning Movement** **Manipulative Skills** **Outdoor Play** pp. 78-79	**Let's Sing:** "Teddy Bear" **Morning Movement** **Manipulative Skills** **Outdoor Play** pp. 78-79	**Morning Movement** **Manipulative Skills** **Outdoor Play** pp. 78-79

C Squared Studios/Getty Images

DIFFERENTIATED INSTRUCTION

	DAY 1	DAY 2
3-Year-Olds and Extra Support	**Alphabet Time:** Assess **Book Time:** *I Know a Lot of Things* **Read and Build Basic Vocabulary** **Science:** Oral Language pp. 39, 41, 43	**Alphabet Time:** Assess **Book Time:** *I Know a Lot of Things* **Who? What? Where?** **Science:** Let's Explore Together pp. 47, 49, 51
Transitional K and Advanced Learners	**Alphabet Time:** Assess **Book Time:** *I Know a Lot of Things* **Read, Respond, and Extend Vocabulary** **Science:** Oral Language pp. 39, 41, 43	**Alphabet Time:** Assess **Book Time:** *I Know a Lot of Things* **Retell** **Science:** Extend the Concept pp. 47, 49, 51
English Learners	**Alphabet Time:** Articulation **Action Rhyme** **Book Time:** Preview and Build Basic Vocabulary **Science:** Preteach Basic Words pp. 39, 41, 43	**Alphabet Time:** Review and Assess **Book Time:** Assess Oral Language **Science:** Develop Vocabulary pp. 47, 49, 51
Adaptations for Children with Special Needs	Modifications for Language Delays, Cognitive Delays, and Children on the Autism Spectrum p. 37	Modifications for Language Delays, Cognitive Delays, and Children on the Autism Spectrum p. 37

DIGITAL RESOURCES

Go Digital
- Teacher Resources
- Interactive Games and Activities
- Transitional K Small Group Planner

Digital Flip Charts
Theme and Transition Songs mp3
Morning Movement mp3
Alphabet Song Videos
Theme Book eBooks
Digital Teacher's Edition and Lesson Planner

Digital Flip Charts
Online Handwriting Videos and Resources
Digital Alphabet, Photo, and Concept Cards
Online Science Games

DAY 3

Alphabet Time: Assess
Book Time: Draw About It
Social Studies: Oral Language

pp. 55, 57, 59

Alphabet Time: Assess
Read: *Ready for Kindergarten*
Book Time: Write About It
Social Studies: Oral Language

pp. 55, 57, 59

Alphabet Time: Review and Assess
Book Time: Assess Oral Language
Write About It
Social Studies: Preteach Basic Words

pp. 55, 57, 59

Modifications for Physical Impairments, Vision Impairments, and Speech and Language Impairments

p. 53

DAY 4

Alphabet Time: Assess
Book Time: Build Basic Vocabulary
Social Studies: Let's Explore Together

pp. 63, 65, 67

Alphabet Time: Assess
Reread: *Ready for Kindergarten*
Book Time: Vocabulary Boost
Social Studies: Extend the Concept

pp. 63, 65, 67

Alphabet Time: Review and Assess
Book Time: Assess Oral Language
Social Studies: Develop Vocabulary

pp. 63, 65, 67

Modifications for Physical Impairments, Vision Impairments, and Speech and Language Impairments

p. 53

DAY 5

Alphabet Assess
Book Time: Act It Out
Science/Social Studies: Review

pp. 71, 73, 75

Alphabet Time: Assess
Book Time: Retell
Science/Social Studies: Review

pp. 71, 73, 75

Alphabet Time: Review and Assess
Book Time: Develop Vocabulary Talk About It
Science/Social Studies: Review

pp. 71, 73, 75

Modifications for Behavior, Attention Deficit Disorder, and ADHD

p. 69

Digital Flip Charts
Social-Emotional eBooks
Little Reader eBooks
Digital Alphabet, Photo, Oral Language, and Concept Cards

Digital Flip Charts
Little Reader eBooks
Digital Retelling Cards
Online Social Studies Games

Digital Flip Charts
Online Math Games
Online Literacy Games
Digital Assessment Resources
Digital Student Portfolio

Day 1 Starting Our Day

Ready for Kindergarten

FOCUS QUESTIONS
How do we move our bodies?
What do our bodies need to stay healthy?

☐ Morning Message

- Gather children and sing the theme song "Teddy Bear."

- Remind children that they will be learning more about how we move our bodies, and what we need to stay healthy.

- Write a message to children. Read it aloud, tracking the print. Point out the week's high-frequency word *for*. Allow children time to respond to the question.

> I have a book for you.
> What kinds of books do you like?

☐ Calendar and Daily Schedule

- Ask children what day it is. Write the sentence: Today is (<u>Tuesday</u>). Discuss what day yesterday was and what day tomorrow will be.

- Have children place a square on all the Mondays on the calendar, a circle on all the Tuesdays, and so on. Help children to notice the weekly pattern that repeats itself throughout the month.

- Display and review today's schedule. Point out daily routines, the order of activities, and identify any special events.

- Choose one of the transition activities listed (or one of your own favorites) to move children into the next activity.

(tl) Art'nLera/Shutterstock.com; (t) Fotos International/Archive Photos/Getty Images; (cr) Ken Cavanagh/McGraw-Hill Education

SOCIAL-EMOTIONAL DEVELOPMENT

New Experiences

My First Day

Grow and Learn with Mister Rogers

Objectives Use words to communicate thoughts and feelings; develop memory skills

Materials none

Talk with children about how you felt as a teacher on the first day of school. For example, you could tell them you felt excited and ready to greet them. Invite children to tell you how they felt on the first day of school. Ask: *Do you remember*

- *what you wore on the first day of school?*
- *the other children who were there?*
- *what you had for snack or lunch?*
- *one of your favorite things in the classroom?*

Don't comment as children talk; sometimes it's important to just listen. Some children may not want to share their feelings. Let those children know you care about their feelings, too. Tell children that some of them will be going to kindergarten next year. Talk about what that might be like and how they might feel in a new classroom.

→ Transitions

Theme Song Sing "Teddy Bear" between activities.

→ Sign Language

Teach the signs for *please* and *wait*. Use these for effective classroom management.

please

wait

→ Meal Talk

What is one fun thing we did together this year?

 ## Adaptations for Children with Special Needs

Language Delays, Cognitive Delays, and Children on the Autism Spectrum

- Use a highlighter to make lines and text visually stand out on worksheets and art activities. For example, highlight where a child needs to write his/her name, and/or where to trace or cut out letters, shapes, or pictures.

- Use tape to attach a single piece of paper to the table, or a large sheet of paper to the table. The tape will help stabilize the paper so that it does not move around when children need to work.

WHOLE GROUP

Alphabet Recognition

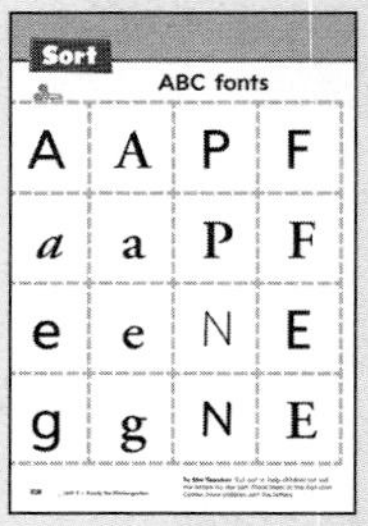
Sort
ABC fonts

A	A	P	F
a	a	P	F
e	e	N	E
g	g	N	E

Objective Alphabet review

Materials Letter Cards, tape, alphabet chart. Teacher's Resource Book p. 108

Letter Review Secure letter cards for all 26 letters on the floor in random order to form a path. Have children hop the path as they say each letter name and sound or sing the Alphabet Song.

ABC Font Sort Distribute copies of Teacher's Resource Book page 108 for children to sort the letters. Discuss each letter's key attributes.

Phonological Awareness

Objective Delete syllables

Materials Photo Cards

Delete Syllables Display a Photo Card (e.g., banana).

- Say the name, then repeat as children clap the syllables (e.g., ba-na-na).
- Then ask children to say the picture name without the first syllable. Children clap and silently mouth the syllable, then say the rest of the word (e.g., clap-na-na).
- Continue with other pictures. Record your observations.

Teacher Table

4-Year-Olds

Objective Assess skills

Materials Assessment Flip Book

Assess Select several children to formally assess each day during Teacher Table time. Administer the Language tests from the Assessment Flip Book individually. Record the results and your observations to determine each child's academic growth throughout the year and to inform the child's kindergarten teacher.

- Use these assessments: Following Directions, Labeling Objects, Position Words, Opposites, Rhyme Recognition, Identifying Same/Different Words, Naming Uppercase Letters, Naming Lowercase Letters, Naming Letter-Sounds, Differentiating Numbers and Letters, Handling a Book.

Alphabet Center

Sound-Matching Games Children match picture cards whose names begin with the same sound. Extend by having them match picture cards with letter cards.

Purposeful Play Prompts *What letter is this? What sound does it make? What words begin with that sound and letter?*

Use the Observation Checklists and Daily Observation Form in the Assessment Handbook to monitor children's progress.

Differentiated Instruction

3-Year-Olds and Extra Support

Objective Assess skills

Materials Assessment Flip Book

Assess Select several children to formally assess each day during Teacher Table time. Administer the Language tests from the Assessment Flip Book individually. Record the results and your observations to determine each child's academic growth throughout the year and to inform the child's next-year teacher.

- Use these assessments: Following Directions, Labeling Objects, Position Words, Opposites, Rhyme Recognition, Identifying Same/Different Words, Naming Uppercase Letters, Naming Lowercase Letters, Naming Letter-Sounds, Differentiating Numbers and Letters, Handling a Book.

Transitional K and Advanced Learners

Objective Assess skills

Materials Assessment Flip Book

Assess Select several children to formally assess each day during Teacher Table time. Administer the Language tests from the Assessment Flip Book individually. Record the results and your observations to determine each child's academic growth throughout the year and to inform the child's kindergarten teacher.

- Use these assessments: Following Directions, Labeling Objects, Position Words, Opposites, Rhyme Recognition, Identifying Same/Different Words, Naming Uppercase Letters, Naming Lowercase Letters, Naming Letter-Sounds, Differentiating Numbers and Letters, Handling a Book.

 English Learners

Objective Review alphabet

Materials Alphabet Song

Review Alphabet Sing the Alphabet Song with children. Then place a set of letter cards on the table.

- Have children take turns collecting the letter cards in their name and others that they recognize.

- Ask them to say the name (and sound, if appropriate) for each letter. Record your observations.

Book Time

CiRCLE TiME
WHOLE GROUP

Read Aloud

Objective Listen and comprehend; learn new vocabulary

Materials *I Know a Lot of Things*

Develop Print Awareness Read the title and names of the author and illustrator as you track the print. Ask children to explain an author and illustrator's role in creating a book.

Read the Book Ask children to listen for things they already know as you read the book.

- Stop every few pages and have children name all the things the story narrator has learned.

Build Vocabulary Use a child-friendly explanation and the pictures to explain the following words: *mirror, wagon, cave, cozy, mushroom, pull, side, wide, bright, round.*

Respond Remind children to take turns listening and speaking as they share their thoughts and questions. Ask:

- *What does the boy know?*
- *What can he do?*
- *What will he learn as he grows?*
- *What will you learn as you grow up?*

Teacher Table

4-Year-Olds

Objective Listen and comprehend; learn new vocabulary

Materials *I Know a Lot of Things*

Revisit Book Reread *I Know a Lot of Things*. Stop on the page with the horse and wagon. Have children find the *horse, wagon,* and *wood* in the picture. Ask: *Which two words begin with the same sound: horse, wagon, wood? What sound do they begin with?* Continue with other pages. Pose alphabet recognition and phonological awareness questions.

Build Vocabulary Review the words introduced in the initial reading. Use the Define-Example-Ask Routine. Then have children name a *cozy* place in the classroom, name something that is *bright* and something that is *round,* and demonstrate how to *pull* something.

Library and Listening Center

Theme-Related Books Provide several "first day of kindergarten" books for children to read or listen to. Help children use the pictures to pretend-read.

Purposeful Play Prompts *How do you hold the book? Where are the words? The pictures? When do you turn the page?*

 Use the Observation Checklists and Daily Observation Form in the Assessment Handbook to monitor children's progress.

Differentiated Instruction

3-Year-Olds and Extra Support

Objective Listen and comprehend; learn new vocabulary

Materials *I Know a Lot of Things*

Develop Print Awareness Read the title and names of the author and illustrator as you track the print. Explain that the author wrote the words. The illustrator drew the pictures.

Reread the Book Ask each child to listen for something the boy knows that they know, too.

Basic Vocabulary Use the pictures to point out the following words: *mirror, horse, ant, snail, wave, hole, climb, square, star.*

Transitional K and Advanced Learners

Objective Listen and comprehend; learn new vocabulary

Materials *I Know a Lot of Things*

Develop Print Awareness Read the title and names of the author and illustrator as you track the print. Ask children what an author and illustrator do in creating a book.

Reread and Respond Ask each child to listen for something the boy knows that they know, too.

Boost Vocabulary Use the pictures and child-friendly explanations to point out the following words: *mirror, wagon, ferry, cave, cozy, acorn, mushroom, pull, side, wide, bright, round.*

 English Learners

Objective Build vocabulary

Materials pictures, *I Know a Lot of Things*

Preview Book Conduct a picture walk of the book. Name the items shown in the pictures. Provide concrete pictures for some of the more abstract pictures, such as *wave* and *cave.*

Focus on Basic Vocabulary Find pictures of the following story nouns: *mirror, wave, cave, wagon, mushroom, star.* Name each picture, and have children repeat. Say a word. Guide children to find the picture and match it to a picture in the book.

Day 1 Science

CIRCLE TIME

WHOLE GROUP

Energy

Objective Discuss energy

Materials Science Flip Chart pp. 75-78, chart paper

Share and Read Create with children a list of different sources of energy they are familiar with. Ask:

- *What types of energy come from the sun?* Point out that we get heat and light from the sun.

- *How are sounds different from each other?* Review how sounds are made (vibrations).

- *How do people use electricity?* Provide examples of electrical items in the classroom.

Read Flip Chart pages 75-78. Stop and discuss children's experiences with energy and electricity. Ask: *What objects do you use to provide light? Where do you hear sounds?*

Build Vocabulary Explain that *energy* is needed for things to move or work. It is the power available to a person, animal, plant, or machine.

Journal Prompt Have children draw a picture of something that uses electricity. Guide them to label the picture.

Energy

Teacher Table

4-Year-Olds

Objective Observe and experiment with motion

Materials toys with wheels, simple machine

How Do We Use Energy?

Observe and Predict Show children a battery-operated toy or appliance. Model how it works. Then remove the batteries. Explain that the batteries give the toy (or appliance) energy, or the power to work. Ask: *What will happen when I turn the toy on now?*

Explore Have children experiment with different forms of energy—from turning on and off light switches, to placing their hands on a ringing and quiet phone.

Science and Discovery Center

Using Energy Give each child a paper divided into four labeled squares: Heat, Light, Electricity, Sound. (See Teacher's Resource Book page 111.) Children draw examples of each type of energy and how they use it.

Purposeful Play Prompts *How do you use electricity at home? Light? What makes sounds?*

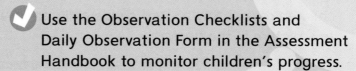 Use the Observation Checklists and Daily Observation Form in the Assessment Handbook to monitor children's progress.

Differentiated Instruction

3-Year-Olds and Extra Support

Objective Use vocabulary associated with energy

Materials toys and classroom objects

Oral Language Have children experiment with different forms of energy—from turning on and off light switches, to placing their hands on a ringing and quiet phone, to playing with battery-operated toys. Introduce the words *energy* and *electricity* to describe what is happening.

Transitional K and Advanced Learners

Objective Discuss energy

Materials toys and classroom objects

Oral Language Show children a battery-operated toy or appliance. Model how it works. Then remove the batteries. Explain that the batteries give the toy (or appliance) *energy*, or the power to work. Ask: *What will happen when I turn the toy on now?*

- Have children experiment with different forms of energy—from turning on and off light switches, to placing their hands on a ringing and quiet phone.

- Guide them to use domain specific language to describe what is happening, such as *energy, sound, vibrations,* and *electricity.*

 **English Learners**

Objective Learn vocabulary

Materials pictures of light switch, radio, computer, and battery-operated toy

Review Basic Words Show children the pictures. Point to each and name it. Have children repeat and demonstrate (where possible). Then introduce the words *energy, electricity,* and *sound.* For example, model turning on a light switch (or a lamp). Say: *The electricity gives us light.* Have children repeat.

Starting Our Day

☐ Welcome

Greet children and prompt them to return a greeting. Guide them to put away and organize their belongings. Remind children to put their name card on the attendance chart.

☐ Morning Message

- Gather children and sing the theme song "Teddy Bear."

- Remind children that they will be learning more about how we move our bodies, and what we need to stay healthy.

- Write a message to children. Read it aloud, tracking the print. Point out the week's high-frequency word *for*. Allow children time to respond to the question.

> I have a surprise for you.
> When have you been surprised?

☐ Calendar and Daily Schedule

- Ask children what day it is. Write the sentence: Today is (Tuesday). Discuss what day yesterday was and what day tomorrow will be.

- Guide children to find the date on the calendar. Help a volunteer to write the date. Have another volunteer read the date. Record the weather on the calendar using a symbol and guide children to see if the weather over the past week has formed a pattern.

- Display and review today's schedule. Point out daily routines, the order of activities, and identify any special events.

- Choose one of the transition activities listed (or one of your own favorites) to move children into the next activity.

SOCIAL-EMOTIONAL DEVELOPMENT

New Experiences

Musical Performances

Grow and Learn
with Mister Rogers

Objectives Appreciate the talents of others;
gain self-control

Materials audio

Ask children if they've ever been to a musical
performance. Explain that it helps to know
ahead of time what to expect. For example,
tell children that audience members:

- sit in their seats before and during the performance.

- try not to talk during a song (that can be hard).

- clap after a song is played.

- wait in their row until it's their turn to leave.

Then invite children to practice being in the audience. Set up a horseshoe-
shaped row of chairs for a "band" and a row for the "audience." Play
instrumental music as the band pretends to play. Turn off the music, and
encourage the audience to clap. After the concert, show children how
to leave their seats.

Health and Safety

Review Health Habits

Objective Review health and safety skills

Materials none

Review the following health habits.

- **Medicine Safety** Ask children who can give them medicine, and where
  medicine should be stored.

- **Healthy Habits** Ask children what they can do to keep germs from
  spreading (e.g., what to do when they need to sneeze or cough).

- **Medical Help** Ask children to explain what doctors and dentists do,
  and why it's important to visit both.

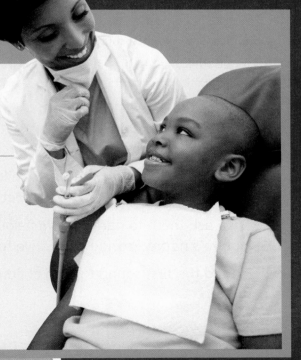

Transitions

Literacy Say a sound (e.g.,
/p/). If the sound matches
the first sound in a child's
name, he or she can line up.
Repeat until all children have
lined up.

Math Have children line up
by counting "as high as they
can." Tap each child lightly
as he or she says the next
number in sequence before
lining up.

Sign Language

Review the signs for *please*
and *wait,* and continue to
use previous signs.

Meal Talk

What songs do you like
to sing?

CiRCLE TiME

WHOLE GROUP

Alphabet Recognition

Objective Alphabet review

Materials Teacher's Resource Book p. 112, dry-erase boards, chart paper

ABC Puzzle Distribute copies of Teacher's Resource Book page 112. Have children cut apart the puzzle pieces, then reassemble the letters in ABC order. Ask them to point to each letter as they say its name.

Write Letters Give children dry-erase boards. Call out a letter. Ask children to write the letter. Then write the letter for children to self-correct. Continue with other letters. Record observations.

Phonological Awareness

Objective Review initial sounds

Materials Photo Cards

Initial Sounds Select 10-12 Photo Cards. Focus on initial vowel sounds. Mix the cards.

- Display one card at a time. Ask children to name the animal, person, or object shown.

- Then ask them to name the first sound in the picture's name. Provide corrective feedback.

- Extend the first sound to help children needing support.

Teacher Table

4-Year-Olds

Objective Assess skills

Materials Assessment Flip Book

Assess Select several children to formally assess each day during Teacher Table time. Administer the Language tests from the Assessment Flip Book individually. Record the results and your observations to determine each child's academic growth throughout the year and to inform the child's kindergarten teacher.

- Use these assessments: Following Directions, Labeling Objects, Position Words, Opposites, Rhyme Recognition, Identifying Same/Different Words, Naming Uppercase Letters, Naming Lowercase Letters, Naming Letter-Sounds, Differentiating Numbers and Letters, Handling a Book.

Alphabet Center

Sound-Matching Games Children match picture cards whose names begin with the same sound. Extend by having them match picture cards with letter cards.

Purposeful Play Prompts *What letter is this? What sound does it make? What words begin with that sound and letter?*

 Use the Observation Checklists and Daily Observation Form in the Assessment Handbook to monitor children's progress.

Differentiated Instruction

3-Year-Olds and Extra Support

Objective Assess skills

Materials Assessment Flip Book

Assess Select several children to formally assess each day during Teacher Table time. Administer the Language tests from the Assessment Flip Book individually. Record the results and your observations to determine each child's academic growth throughout the year and to inform the child's next-year teacher.

- Use these assessments: Following Directions, Labeling Objects, Position Words, Opposites, Rhyme Recognition, Identifying Same/Different Words, Naming Uppercase Letters, Naming Lowercase Letters, Naming Letter-Sounds, Differentiating Numbers and Letters, Handling a Book.

Transitional K and Advanced Learners

Objective Assess skills

Materials Assessment Flip Book

Assess Select several children to formally assess each day during Teacher Table time. Administer the Language tests from the Assessment Flip Book individually. Record the results and your observations to determine each child's academic growth throughout the year and to inform the child's kindergarten teacher.

- Use these assessments: Following Directions, Labeling Objects, Position Words, Opposites, Rhyme Recognition, Identifying Same/Different Words, Naming Uppercase Letters, Naming Lowercase Letters, Naming Letter-Sounds, Differentiating Numbers and Letters, Handling a Book.

Ken Cavanagh/McGraw-Hill Education

EL English Learners

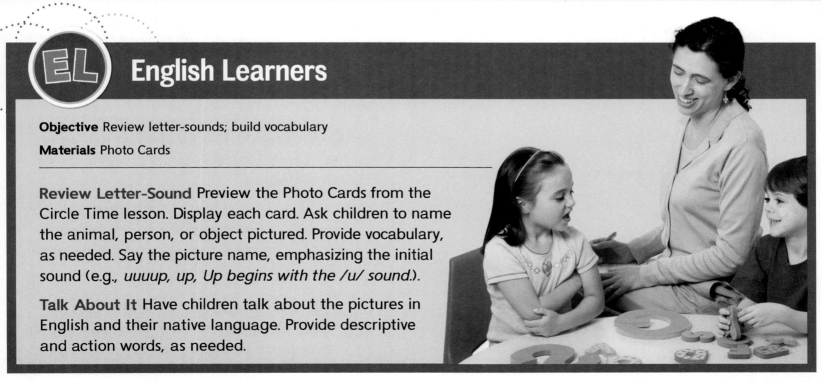

Objective Review letter-sounds; build vocabulary

Materials Photo Cards

Review Letter-Sound Preview the Photo Cards from the Circle Time lesson. Display each card. Ask children to name the animal, person, or object pictured. Provide vocabulary, as needed. Say the picture name, emphasizing the initial sound (e.g., *uuuup, up, Up begins with the /u/ sound.*).

Talk About It Have children talk about the pictures in English and their native language. Provide descriptive and action words, as needed.

Day 2 Book Time

CIRCLE TIME

WHOLE GROUP

Reread

Objective Begin to compare and contrast

Materials I *Know a Lot of Things*

Focus on Compare and Contrast Reread the book. Create a list of ten things the boy in the book knows. Ask: *How many of these things did you already know?*

- *Have children write their name beside three things they know on the list.*

- *Count the number of names beside each item.*

- *Guide children to determine which thing the most and least number of children knew.*

Journal Prompt Have children draw a picture of one thing they hope to learn in kindergarten. Guide children to write a sentence for their picture. If children dictate a sentence, share the pen for letters and words they know.

Teacher Table

4-Year-Olds

Objective Begin to retell information learned

Materials I *Know a Lot of Things*

Model Retelling Page through the book and model retelling key details. Then guide children in retelling key details. Have them flip through the pages and state what the boy knows. Guide them to express their ideas in complete sentences.

Library and Listening Center

Theme-Related Books Provide several "first day of kindergarten" books for children to read or listen to. Help children use the pictures to pretend-read.

Focus on Speaking/Listening Guide children to express ideas and opinions about the books in complete sentences. Model by restating children's statements.

 Use the Observation Checklists and Daily Observation Form in the Assessment Handbook to monitor children's progress.

Differentiated Instruction

3-Year-Olds and Extra Support

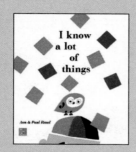

Objective Identify details

Materials *I Know a Lot of Things*

Details Reread the book. As you page through it, stop and ask basic *What?* detail questions.

- *What does the boy see when he looks in the mirror?*
- *What sound does a cat make? A dog? Why?*
- *What can a horse do?*

Transitional K and Advanced Learners

Objective Retell information learned; expand ideas

Materials *I Know a Lot of Things*

Retell Reread the book. Then flip through it as children take turns retelling the key details using the illustrations and what they recall from listening carefully. Work with children to expand ideas by providing additional descriptive details (e.g., juicy, red, ripe berry). Model adding details to sentences and combining ideas as you restate children's oral responses.

Partner Read Allow partners to flip through the book. Prompt them to retell key details and share personal responses to the story. Listen in and note children's use of language (vocabulary) and sentence structures.

 **English Learners**

Objective Assess language

Materials *Tell Me About It*, tape recorder

Assess Oral Language Individually, give each child a copy of *Tell Me About It* (nonfiction). Have the child page through the book, examine the photos, and tell as many details as possible about each worker. Tape record the retelling. Then transcribe the recording and place in the child's portfolio as a record of their growing language skills.

Day 2 Science

CIRCLE TIME

WHOLE GROUP

Energy

Objective Discuss energy

Materials Science Flip Chart pp. 75-78, chart paper

Share and Read Review with children the list of different sources of energy they created in the last lesson. Ask:

- *What types of energy come from the sun?* Review that we get heat and light from the sun.

- *How are sounds different from each other?* Review how sounds are made (vibrations).

- *How do people use electricity?* Provide additional examples of electrical items in the classroom.

Reread Flip Chart pages 75-78. Ask: *What objects do you use to provide light? Where do you hear sounds? What objects use electricity in our classroom or at your home?*

Build Vocabulary Review that *energy* is needed for things to move or work. It is the power available to a person, animal, plant, or machine.

Energy

Teacher Table

4-Year-Olds

Objective Observe and experiment with motion

Materials toys with wheels, simple machine

How Do We Use Energy?

Observe and Predict Show children another battery-operated toy or appliance. Model how it works. Then remove the batteries. Review that the batteries give the toy (or appliance) energy, or the power to work. Ask: *What will happen when I turn the toy on now?*

Explore Have children continue to experiment with different forms of energy—from turning on and off light switches, to placing their hands on a ringing and quiet phone.

Science and Discovery Center

Using Energy Children continue to draw examples of each type of energy: Heat, Light, Electricity, Sound.

Focus on Listening/Speaking Guide children to use conversational rules when discussing concepts with you, such as listening without interrupting. Stop and model, as needed.

✓ Use the Observation Checklists and Daily Observation Form in the Assessment Handbook to monitor children's progress.

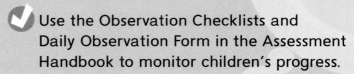

Differentiated Instruction

3-Year-Olds and Extra Support

Objective Use vocabulary associated with energy

Materials toys and classroom items

Oral Language Have children continue to experiment with different forms of energy—from turning on and off light switches, to placing their hands on a ringing and quiet phone, to playing with battery-operated toys. Review the words *energy* and *electricity* to describe what is happening.

Transitional K and Advanced Learners

Objective Discuss energy

Materials toys and classroom items

Oral Language Show children another battery-operated toy or appliance. Model how it works. Then remove the batteries. Remind children that the batteries give the toy (or appliance) *energy*, or the power to work. Ask: *What will happen when I turn the toy on now?*

- Have children continue to experiment with different forms of energy—from turning on and off light switches, to placing their hands on a ringing and quiet phone.

- Guide them to use domain specific language to describe what is happening, such as *energy, sound, vibrations,* and *electricity.*

 ## English Learners

Objective Develop concept vocabulary

Materials Concept Cards, online games

Develop Vocabulary Use the Concept Cards and online science games to develop children's theme-related vocabulary. Have children play the games independently and with partners. The visual and audio supports reinforce and build word knowledge. Use the photo to play matching and sorting games. Identify each picture name and have children repeat before, during, and after play.

SCIENCE GAMES

Day 3 Starting Our Day

☐ Welcome

Greet children by singing the "Hello Song" or another favorite greeting song. Guide children to put away and organize their belongings. Prompt children to put their name card on the attendance chart.

☐ Morning Message

- Gather children and sing the theme song "Teddy Bear."

- Remind children that they will be learning more about how we move our bodies, and what we need to stay healthy.

- Write a message to children. Read it aloud, tracking the print. Point out the week's high-frequency word *for*. Allow children time to respond to the question.

> *I like to exercise each day.*
> *What can I do for exercise?*

☐ Calendar and Daily Schedule

- Ask children what day it is. Write the sentence: Today is (Wednesday). Discuss what day yesterday was and what day tomorrow will be.

- Guide children to record the weather using a symbol, such as a sun or a cloud. Ask: *What kind of clothing do we need for today's weather?*

- Display and review today's schedule. Point out daily routines, the order of activities, and identify any special events.

- Choose one of the transition activities listed (or one of your own favorites) to move children into the next activity.

100   Ready for Kindergarten

SOCIAL-EMOTIONAL DEVELOPMENT

Review

Objective Listen to a read aloud
Materials Social-Emotional Read Alouds

Read and Reflect Display all eight Social-Emotional Read Alouds. Guide children to revisit the covers. Track the print as you read each title.

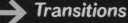

- Tell children that they have learned a lot about how to act in school and be a good friend, and that they can feel proud of their accomplishments.

- Guide children to tell one way they learned to be a good friend or make good choices in school.

- Explain to children how a kindergarten classroom is similar to and different from their classroom. Reassure them that they are ready for next year.

Journal Prompt Have children draw a picture showing how they act in school. Ask them to write or dictate a sentence for their picture.

(tl) Art'nLera/Shutterstock.com

→ *Transitions*

Literacy Have children clap the syllables in their name as they line up.

Math Place number cards 2-10 on the floor in sequence. Have each child line up next to the number that matches the number of letters in his or her first name.

→ *Sign Language*

Review the signs for *please* and *wait,* and continue to use previous signs.

→ *Meal Talk*

What makes a good friend?

Adaptations for Children with Special Needs

Physical, Vision, and Speech and Language Impairments

- Use foam sheets to help children grasp the handles of fine motor instruments (pencils, crayons, paintbrushes, forks, shovels, etc.). Wrap the foam sheet around the instrument, and secure with duct or painter's tape.

- Use black or yellow laminated sheets to add high contrast for choice making. Place objects or pictures of contrasting colors on the sheet and ask the child to choose one. Vary the number of choices based on the child's ability to scan more than one at a time.

CiRCLE TiME
WHOLE GROUP

Alphabet Recognition

Objective Review Alphabet

Materials Letter Cards, paper, pencils, crayons, finger paint

Letter-Sound Review Hide (easily visible) letter cards around the room. Have children find them and name each letter and its sound. Discuss each letter's attributes (e.g., curves, straight lines, name).

Write Letters Have children sort letter cards by attribute (e.g., letters formed with all straight lines). Once the sets are formed, have children write the letters from each set on separate sheets of paper. Children can use pencils, crayons, or finger paint.

Print Awareness

Objective Recognize sentences

Materials chart paper

Sentences Write the sentence *I like to read.*

> I like to read.

- Say: *This sentence has four words. Watch as I point to each word and count it. Now it's your turn. Count with me: 1, 2, 3, 4.*

- Then point out that the first word in a sentence begins with a capital, or uppercase, letter. Circle the capital *I*. Also point out the period at the end of the sentence. Repeat with other sentences.

Teacher Table

4-Year-Olds

Objective Assess skills

Materials Assessment Flip Book

Assess Select several children to formally assess each day during Teacher Table time. Administer the Language tests from the Assessment Flip Book individually. Record the results and your observations to determine each child's academic growth throughout the year and to inform the child's kindergarten teacher.

- Use these assessments: Following Directions, Labeling Objects, Position Words, Opposites, Rhyme Recognition, Identifying Same/Different Words, Naming Uppercase Letters, Naming Lowercase Letters, Naming Letter-Sounds, Differentiating Numbers and Letters, Handling a Book.

Alphabet Center

Build a Name Children use magnetic letters, letter cards, clay, art supplies, and other resources to form their names.

Focus on Grammar Model how to create longer sentences by combining children's ideas.

✔ Use the Observation Checklists and Daily Observation Form in the Assessment Handbook to monitor children's progress.

Differentiated Instruction

3-Year-Olds and Extra Support

Objective Assess skills

Materials Assessment Flip Book

Assess Select several children to formally assess each day during Teacher Table time. Administer the Language tests from the Assessment Flip Book individually. Record the results and your observations to determine each child's academic growth throughout the year and to inform the child's next-year teacher.

- Use these assessments: Following Directions, Labeling Objects, Position Words, Opposites, Rhyme Recognition, Identifying Same/Different Words, Naming Uppercase Letters, Naming Lowercase Letters, Naming Letter-Sounds, Differentiating Numbers and Letters, Handling a Book.

Transitional K and Advanced Learners

Objective Substitute sounds; read text

Materials Photo Cards, *Will You Go With Me?*

Substitute Sounds Display Photo Cards for *fan, man,* and *moon.* Tell children you want to replace the first sound in *fan* with /m/ to make a new word, then find the matching picture. Model. Repeat with other picture sets.

Reread *Will You Go With Me?* Have children individually read the book to you.

- Monitor children's reading abilities (noting which types of words give them difficulties and how they handle the book) and record your observations.

- Ask children to give a 1-2 sentence summary of the book. Say: *Tell me what this book is about in just a few words.*

Ken Cavanagh/McGraw-Hill Education

EL English Learners

Objective Build theme-related vocabulary

Materials Oral Language Cards (145-150)

Oral Language Display the sports Oral Language Cards. Name each picture and have children repeat. Then say the name of a piece of sports equipment, and have children find the matching picture card.

Write About It Have children select a card and draw a picture of themselves using that piece of sports equipment. Help them add a label.

English-Spanish helmet/casco, ball/pelota, jump rope/saltar de cuerda

Day 3 Book Time

Teacher Table

4-Year-Olds

Objective Write a sentence

Materials *I Know a Lot of Things*, paper, pencils

Write About It Have children create a sentence stating something they want to know or learn how to do.

- Remind children that a sentence begins with a capital letter and ends with an end mark. Since these sentences are telling sentences, they will end with a period.

- Guide children to write their sentence.

- Children can dictate their sentence. Share the pen for letters (e.g., the initial letter of a word) and words they know.

CiRCLE TiME
WHOLE GROUP

Shared Writing

Objective Use *I* to write a sentence

Materials chart paper, marker, *I Know a Lot of Things*

Write a Sentence with I Flip through the book. Have children find the word *I* on several pages.

- Write one of the sentences on the chart, such as *I know a cat goes meow.* Prompt children to circle the word *I.*

- Tell children you want to work together to write a sentence telling what each of them know, beginning with the word *I.*

- Provide and write the sentence frame *I know.* Write what children dictate. Share the pen, as appropriate.

> ### I Know a Lot
> I know how to read.

Writing and Drawing Center

Pre-Writing Technique Model line strokes that children struggle with. Observe and provide corrective feedback as children write. Additional handwriting resources are available online.

Purposeful Play Prompts Ask children: *How do you hold your pencil? What sound does the word begin with? What letter do you write for that sound?*

 Use the Observation Checklists and Daily Observation Form in the Assessment Handbook to monitor children's progress.

Differentiated Instruction

3-Year-Olds and Extra Support

Objective Write (draw/create) a personal response

Materials *I Know a Lot of Things*

Draw About It Have children draw a picture of something they want to know or learn how to do. Ask them to write their name under their picture. Then write the label or sentence children dictate for their picture.

Transitional K and Advanced Learners

Objective Write a personal response

Materials *I Know a Lot of Things*

Write About It Have children write about something they want to know or learn how to do. Children can flip through *I Know a Lot of Things* for ideas.

- Remind children that a sentence begins with a capital letter and ends with an end mark. Since these sentences are telling sentences, they will end with a period.

- Guide children to write their sentence.

- Prompt them to write words they learned this year and the correct initial and final letters of each word in their sentence (where appropriate).

 **English Learners**

Objective Assess language

Materials *Tell Me About It,* tape recorder

Assess Oral Language Individually, give each child a copy of *Tell Me About It* (nonfiction). Have the child page through the book, examine the pictures, and tell as many details about the photos as possible. Tape record the retelling. Then transcribe the recording and place in the child's portfolio as a record of their growing language skills.

Social Studies

CiRCLE TiME

WHOLE GROUP

Exercise Is Fun!

Objective Learn about different types of exercise

Materials Social Studies Flip Chart p. 50, audio

Share and Read Have children sing and perform the actions of "Clap Your Hands." (For complete song lyrics, see Read-Aloud Anthology page 135.)

- **Vocabulary** Display the Flip Chart and read the question. Use a child-friendly explanation and the photos to point out the word *exercise*.

- Have children describe what they see in the photographs and then discuss. Remind them that you can exercise with friends or family, or by yourself.

- Ask: *What are your favorite types of exercise?*

Social Studies
How do we exercise?

Unit 10 • Ready for Kindergarten   50

Exercise Is Fun!

Teacher Table

4-Year-Olds

Objective Learn about different types of exercise

Materials exercise equipment (e.g., balls, jump ropes)

Draw It Display various exercise equipment. Ask children how each is used. If time permits, go outside for children to demonstrate.

- Then have children draw pictures of themselves using their favorite exercise equipment. Discuss the health benefits and any safety rules.

- Help them label their pictures. If children dictate the label, guide them to identify the first sound in the word and write that letter.

Social Studies Center

Doctor Provide props, such as a plastic doctor's kit with stethoscope, for children to pretend playing doctor.

Purposeful Play Prompts Work with children to use specific health-related words as they share what they're doing in the center. *What do you do with a stethoscope? How does a doctor help you?*

✓ Use the Observation Checklists and Daily Observation Form in the Assessment Handbook to monitor children's progress.

Differentiated Instruction

3-Year-Olds and Extra Support

Objective Learn about different types of exercise

Materials exercise equipment (e.g., balls, jump ropes)

Oral Language Display various exercise equipment. Ask children how each is used. If time permits, go outside for children to demonstrate.

- Then have children draw pictures of themselves using their favorite exercise equipment.

- Have them dictate labels for you to write on their pictures.

Transitional K and Advanced Learners

Objective Learn about different types of exercise

Materials exercise equipment (e.g., balls, jump ropes)

Oral Language Display various exercise equipment. Ask children how each is used. If time permits, go outside for children to demonstrate.

- Then have children draw pictures of themselves using their favorite exercise equipment.

- Help them label their pictures, then write a sentence about why exercise is important.

- Guide them to identify sounds in the words and write the corresponding letters (e.g., initial and final letter-sounds they have learned).

 **English Learners**

Objective Learn vocabulary

Materials Concept Cards (165-169)

Review Basic Words Show children the health-related Concept Cards. Point to each and name it (e.g., *eating*). Pantomime an action. Have children find the matching photo and name it. Provide sentence frames for children to talk about the pictures (e.g., *He/She is ____.*).

Starting Our Day

☐ ## Welcome

Greet children and guide them to put away and organize their belongings. Prompt children to put their name card on the attendance chart.

☐ ## Morning Message

- Gather children and sing the theme song "Teddy Bear."

- Remind children that they will be learning more about how we grow and change, and how we stay healthy.

- Write a message to children. Read it aloud, tracking the print. Point out any uppercase letters and end punctuation. Allow children time to respond to the question.

> *We read a lot of books!*
> *Which book was your favorite?*

☐ ## Calendar and Daily Schedule

- Ask children what day it is. Write the sentence: Today is (Thursday). Discuss what day yesterday was and what day tomorrow will be.

- Sing the "Days of the Week" song. Guide children to find the letter or alphabet card that matches the first letter of the day's name (e.g., W). Count with children the number of letters in the day's name.

- Display and review today's schedule. Point out daily routines, the order of activities, and identify any special events.

- Choose one of the transition activities listed (or one of your own favorites) to move children into the next activity.

SOCIAL-EMOTIONAL DEVELOPMENT

Review

Objective Listen to a read aloud

Materials Social-Emotional Read Alouds

Reread and Reflect Distribute the books, one book per small group of children. Prompt children to talk with their friends about the stories and what they remember.

- Throughout the week, take pictures of children making good choices, being good friends, solving problems with words, and showing respect. Share and discuss the photos with children. Invite them to reflect on how they can make good choices each day.

- As children collaborate, encourage them to identify their preferences when making choices and listening to others before speaking.

(tl) Art'nLera/Shutterstock.com

→ Transitions

Music/Movement Sing children's favorite songs from the year to review them and transition between activities.

→ Sign Language

Review the signs for *please* and *wait*, and continue to use previous signs.

→ Meal Talk

What are you proud of learning this year?

Health and Safety

Review Health Habits

Objective Review health and safety skills

Materials none

Review the following health habits.

- **Medicine Safety** Ask children who can give them medicine, and where medicine should be stored.

- **Healthy Habits** Ask children what they can do to keep germs from spreading (e.g., what to do when they need to sneeze or cough).

- **Medical Help** Ask children to explain what doctors and dentists do, and why it's important to visit both.

Day 4 Alphabet Time

CiRCLE TiME

WHOLE GROUP

High-Frequency Word

Objective Read and write high-frequency words

Materials chart paper

Teach *for* Use the Read-Spell-Write Routine to teach *for*.

- **Read** Write the word *for*. Point to it. Say: *This is the word* for. *What is the word?*

- **Spell** Point to each letter and say its name. Repeat and have children join in. Say: For *is spelled* f-o-r.

- **Write** Have children write the word (or trace it) as they say each letter name.

Alphabet Recognition

Objective Read connected text; recognize high-frequency words

Materials *Ready for Kindergarten*

Read *Ready for Kindergarten*
Read the title. Have children repeat.

- Review left-to-right progression and page turning. Have children point to the spaces between words.

- Preview the book's pattern: *We can ____.*

- Tell children to point to each word as they chorally read the book with you. Read the book twice.

Check Comprehension Ask: *What can the children do? Which of these things can you do?*

Teacher Table

4-Year-Olds

Objective Assess skills

Materials Assessment Flip Book

Assess Select several children to formally assess each day during Teacher Table time. Administer the Language tests from the Assessment Flip Book individually. Record the results and your observations to determine each child's academic growth throughout the year and to inform the child's kindergarten teacher.

- Use these assessments: Following Directions, Labeling Objects, Position Words, Opposites, Rhyme Recognition, Identifying Same/Different Words, Naming Uppercase Letters, Naming Lowercase Letters, Naming Letter-Sounds, Differentiating Numbers and Letters, Handling a Book.

Alphabet Center

Alphabet Puzzles Stock the center with alphabet puzzles. Sing the Alphabet Song with children, pointing to each letter in the puzzle. Prompt children to point to and name letters they know.

Focus on Grammar Model how to create longer sentences by combining children's ideas.

 Use the Observation Checklists and Daily Observation Form in the Assessment Handbook to monitor children's progress.

Differentiated Instruction

3-Year-Olds and Extra Support

Objective Assess skills

Materials Assessment Flip Book

Assess Select several children to formally assess each day during Teacher Table time. Administer the Language tests from the Assessment Flip Book individually. Record the results and your observations to determine each child's academic growth throughout the year and to inform the child's next-year teacher.

- Use these assessments: Following Directions, Labeling Objects, Position Words, Opposites, Rhyme Recognition, Identifying Same/Different Words, Naming Uppercase Letters, Naming Lowercase Letters, Naming Letter Sounds, Differentiating Numbers and Letters, Handling a Book.

Transitional K and Advanced Learners

Objective Read connected text

Materials Letter Cards, word cards, *Will You Go With Me?*

Letter-Sound Review Use letter cards to review letter-sounds. Then display word cards for children to blend: *cat, am, on, pot, it, big, let, red, up, run.*

Reread *Will You Go With Me?* Have children reread the book to a partner to build fluency.

- Listen in and record observations.

- **Write** Have children create a list of things they want to learn in kindergarten. As an alternative, have them write about their favorite book they read this year and state a reason for their opinion. Provide a sentence frame: *I liked ___ because ___.*

 **English Learners**

Objective Build vocabulary

Materials Concept Cards (165–169)

Review Basic Words Review the health-related Concept Cards. Pantomime an action. Have children find the matching picture and name it. Provide sentence frames for children to talk about the pictures (e.g., *He/She is ___.*).

Talk About It Give each child the card pile. Have children act out one card for their classmates to guess the action.

Day 4 Book Time

CiRCLE TiME

WHOLE GROUP

Classic Tale

Objective Listen and comprehend; learn new vocabulary

Materials Retelling Cards; Read-Aloud Anthology p. 96

The Turtle and the Flute
Display the first Retelling Card and have children discuss the illustration. Then read the story and have them listen to find out what happens when the turtle is taken away from its home. Display the other cards as prompted.

Respond Have children try to imagine what Turtle's music sounds like. Have them hum or use instruments to make this music.

Teacher Table

4-Year-Olds

Objective Learn new vocabulary
Materials Retelling Cards

Revisit Tale Display the Retelling Cards for "The Turtle and the Flute" and guide children to put them in order. Have children describe what is happening in each scene. Ask: *Where is Turtle? Why is Turtle scared?*

Build Vocabulary Explain the words *joyful, entertain,* and *returned* using the Define-Example-Ask Routine.

- **Define** *Joyful* means "very happy."

- **Example** *The Browns are a very joyful family. They love to have fun.*

- **Ask** *What makes you feel joyful?*

Writing and Drawing Center

Theme Draw/Write Children continue to write about the many things they accomplished this year in school—things they are proud of.

Purposeful Play Prompts Ask children: *What are you drawing or writing about?* Write labels and sentences they dictate for their drawings to review that print conveys meaning.

 Use the Observation Checklists and Daily Observation Form in the Assessment Handbook to monitor children's progress.

Differentiated Instruction

3-Year-Olds and Extra Support

Objective Learn new vocabulary

Materials Retelling Cards

Revisit Tale Display the Retelling Cards for "The Turtle and the Flute" and guide children to put them in order.

Basic Vocabulary Use the illustrated scenes to build basic vocabulary. Prompt children to point to various characters, actions, and things as you name them. Use descriptive words when naming them, such as "the scared turtle" or the "laughing children." Then name an item or character pictured and have children find and describe it (e.g., *Find the turtle. Tell me about her.*).

Transitional K and Advanced Learners

Objective Learn new vocabulary

Materials Retelling Cards

Revisit Tale Display the Retelling Cards for "The Turtle and the Flute" and guide children to put them in order. Ask: *Where is Turtle? How does she feel?*

Vocabulary Boost Explain the words *joyful, entertain, returned, banks, cage, far,* and *mention,* using the Define-Example-Ask Routine.

- Point out that the work *bank* has two meanings. Children have learned that a bank is a place where people put their money. The word *bank* also means the edge of a river where the water meets the dry soil or sand.

- As you read other books, look for common words children know that are used in a new way.

EL English Learners

Objective Build vocabulary

Materials pictures, Retelling Cards, "The Turtle and the Flute"

Preview Story Display the three Retelling Cards, one at a time. Use simple vocabulary and gestures as you tell the story. Use 1-2 sentences per card. Point to characters and objects as you name them, such as the turtle, riverbank, children, and flute.

Focus on Basic Vocabulary Find pictures of the following story words: *turtle, flute, cage, soup, laughed.* Name each picture, and have children repeat. Play I Spy. Say a word (e.g., *I spy _____.*). Guide children to find the picture and say the picture name as they pick it up.

Ken Cavanagh/McGraw-Hill Education

CIRCLE TIME
WHOLE GROUP

What Our Bodies Need

Objective Learn about different types of exercise

Materials Social Studies Flip Chart p. 50, audio

Share and Read Have children sing and perform the actions of "Clap Your Hands." (For complete song lyrics, see Read-Aloud Anthology page 135.)

- **Vocabulary** Display the Flip Chart and review the photos and the meaning of the word *exercise*.

- Remind children that you can exercise with friends or family, or by yourself. Ask: *When was the last time you exercised? What did you do?*

- Discuss with children why exercise in important. Have them create new words and movements for the song "Clap Your Hands," such as *Ride, ride, ride your bike*. Then sing and act out the new verses.

Journal Prompt *What are your favorite ways to exercise?*

Exercise Is Fun

Teacher Table

4-Year-Olds

Objective Learn about different types of exercise

Materials exercise equipment (e.g., balls, jump ropes)

Draw It Continue to display various exercise equipment. Ask children how each is used. If time permits, go outside for children to demonstrate.

- Then have children continue to draw pictures of themselves using their favorite exercise equipment. Review the health benefits and any safety rules.

- Help them label their pictures. If children dictate the label, guide them to identify the first sound in the word and write that letter.

Social Studies Center

Doctor Provide props, such as a plastic doctor's kit, for children to pretend playing doctor.

Focus on Listening/Speaking Guide children to use conversational rules when discussing concepts with you, such as listening without interrupting, turn-taking, and using appropriate intonation. Stop and model, as needed.

 Use the Observation Checklists and Daily Observation Form in the Assessment Handbook to monitor children's progress.

Differentiated Instruction

3-Year-Olds and Extra Support

Objective Learn about different types of exercise

Materials exercise equipment (e.g., balls, jump ropes)

Oral Language Continue to display various exercise equipment. Ask children how each is used. If time permits, go outside for children to demonstrate.

- Then have children continue to draw pictures of themselves using their favorite exercise equipment.

- Have them dictate labels for you to write on their pictures.

Transitional K and Advanced Learners

Objective Learn about different types of exercise

Materials exercise equipment (e.g., balls, jump ropes)

Oral Language Continue to display various exercise equipment. Ask children how each is used. If time permits, go outside for children to demonstrate.

- Then have children continue to draw pictures of themselves using their favorite exercise equipment.

- Help them label their pictures, then write a sentence about why exercise is important. Guide them to identify sounds in the words and write the corresponding letters (e.g., initial and final letter-sounds they have learned).

 English Learners

Objective Develop concept vocabulary

Materials Concept Cards, online games

Develop Vocabulary Use the Concept Cards and online social studies games to develop children's theme-related vocabulary. Have children play the games independently and with partners. The visual and audio supports reinforce and build word knowledge. Use the cards to play matching and sorting games. Identify each picture name and have children repeat before, during, and after play.

SOCIAL STUDIES GAMES

Starting Our Day

☐ ## Welcome

Greet children and help them to make eye contact with you as they return a greeting. Guide them to put away and organize their belongings. Prompt children to put their name card on the attendance chart.

☐ ## Morning Message

- Gather children and sing the theme song "Teddy Bear."

- Remind children that they will be learning more about how we move our bodies, and what we need to stay healthy.

- Write a message to children. Read it aloud, tracking the print. Have children point out any letters and words they know. Contrast letters with numbers when looking at the calendar. Allow children time to respond to the last statement.

You have been great students. I will miss you all!

☐ ## Calendar and Daily Schedule

- Ask children what day it is. Write the sentence: Today is (Friday). Discuss what day yesterday was and what day tomorrow will be.

- Review the days of the week using the "Days of the Week" song. Clap out the syllables of each day's name as you say it.

- Display and review today's schedule. Point out daily routines, the order of activities, and identify any special events.

- Choose one of the transition activities listed (or one of your own favorites) to move children into the next activity.

SOCIAL-EMOTIONAL DEVELOPMENT

Making Good Choices

Objective Discuss making good choices at school

Materials Social-Emotional Flip Chart

1 Make Good Choices Display the Social-Emotional Flip Chart. Flip through the pages and stop on any concepts children need to review.

- Examine the picture with children and ask the questions provided.

- Complete any projects (writing, creating artwork, or acting out scenes) related to the Flip Chart page you didn't have time to address earlier in the year.

- Have children re-enact the page, modeling how to act or respond in the situation pictured.

WEEKLY TIP Compliment children on how they have grown and changed throughout the year.

→ **Transitions**
Your Choice

_____
_____
_____
_____

→ **Sign Language**
Review the signs for *please* and *wait*, and continue to use previous signs.

→ **Meal Talk**
What will you be doing this summer?

 ## Adaptations for Children with Special Needs

Behavior Problems, Attention Deficit Disorder, and ADHD

- Create a turn-taking prop, or a visual reminder of whose turn it is. Use glue to attach a craft stick to a foam sheet. During a turn-taking activity, such as Circle Time, the child who is holding the prop takes his/her turn while the others wait.

- Use verbal and visual cues to help children anticipate transitions. Ten minutes before the end of an activity, announce "ten minutes left" while holding up ten fingers. Then follow with five-minute and two-minute warnings.

CiRCLE TiME

WHOLE GROUP

Alphabet Recognition

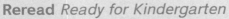

Objective Read a theme-related book

Materials *Ready for Kindergarten*

Reread *Ready for Kindergarten*
Point to the high-frequency words
with and *for* on the pages. Have children say them aloud. Then tell them to point to each word as they chorally read it with you. Read the book twice.

- **Retell** Invite children to retell what they learned to a partner, using the photos.

- **Talk About It** Have children tell what they can do now that they couldn't at the beginning of the school year.

High-Frequency Word

Objective Read and write high-frequency words

Materials chart paper

Review *for* Use the Read-Spell-Write Routine to review *for*.

- **Read** Write the word *for*. Point to it. Say: *This is the word* for. *What is the word?*

- **Spell** Point to each letter and say its name. Repeat and have children join in. Say: For *is spelled* f-o-r.

- **Write** Have children write or trace the word as they say each letter name, then create oral sentences with *for*. Write their sentences. Share the pen.

Teacher Table

4-Year-Olds

Objective Assess skills

Materials Assessment Flip Book

Assess Select several children to formally assess each day during Teacher Table time. Administer the Language tests from the Assessment Flip Book individually. Record the results and your observations to determine each child's academic growth throughout the year and to inform the child's kindergarten teacher.

- Use these assessments: Following Directions, Labeling Objects, Position Words, Opposites, Rhyme Recognition, Identifying Same/Different Words, Naming Uppercase Letters, Naming Lowercase Letters, Naming Letter-Sounds, Differentiating Numbers and Letters, Handling a Book.

Alphabet Center

Alphabet Fun Use the online literacy games to develop children's skills. Have children play the games independently and with partners. The visual and audio supports reinforce and build letter knowledge and phonemic awareness.

 Use the Observation Checklists and Daily Observation Form in the Assessment Handbook to monitor children's progress.

Differentiated Instruction

3-Year-Olds and Extra Support

Objective Assess skills

Materials Assessment Flip Book

Assess Select several children to formally assess each day during Teacher Table time. Administer the Language tests from the Assessment Flip Book individually. Record the results and your observations to determine each child's academic growth throughout the year and to inform the child's next-year teacher.

- Use these assessments: Following Directions, Labeling Objects, Position Words, Opposites, Rhyme Recognition, Identifying Same/Different Words, Naming Uppercase Letters, Naming Lowercase Letters, Naming Letter-Sounds, Differentiating Numbers and Letters, Handling a Book.

Transitional K and Advanced Learners

Objective Write words with short vowels

Materials word cards, letter cards

Write Words with Short Vowels Display word cards for children to blend: *can, am, on, top, it, big, let, red, up, run.*

- Then guide children to write each word. Model segmenting the word sound-by-sound and attaching a letter to each sound.

- For children needing support, give them the letter cards needed to form the word. Guide them to place the letter cards in order as you say each sound in the word.

EL English Learners

Objective Build theme-related vocabulary

Materials Oral Language Cards

Oral Language Display the Oral Language Cards from the year. Put them in small piles on the table.

- Have children go through each pile and name and describe the pictures. Monitor their use of vocabulary and sentence structure.

- Prompt children to tell as much as they can about the pictures. Record your observations.

Ken Cavanagh/McGraw-Hill Education

Book Time

CiRCLE TiME

WHOLE GROUP • READ ALOUD

Classic Tale

Objective Listen and comprehend; begin to retell story events

Materials Retelling Cards; Read-Aloud Anthology p. 96

Reread and Model Retelling
Reread the story. Use the Retelling Cards to model a retelling. Then guide children in identifying the setting; telling who the characters are; and describing what happens first, next, and so on. Use a sequence graphic organizer to record these events as children state them.

Journal Prompt Have children draw a picture from the story and write a retelling. Have them dictate sentences to describe their picture. Review that the sentence begins with an uppercase, or capital, letter, and ends with the correct punctuation mark.

Teacher Table

4-Year-Olds

Objective Listen and retell; practice new vocabulary

Materials Retelling Cards; Read-Aloud Anthology p. 96

Guided Retell Place the Retelling Cards on the table. Have children take turns putting them in the proper sequence (beginning, middle, end). Then have children retell the story using the pictures. Listen in and direct children to provide missing details. Prompt them using the questions on the back of each card.

Dramatic Play
Center

Kindergarten Take children to visit their next year's kindergarten class. Afterward, have them describe what is the same and different. Have them "play" kindergarten.

Focus on Speaking Focus children on speaking clearly and in complete sentences with proper subject-verb agreement. Model, as needed.

✓ Use the Observation Checklists and Daily Observation Form in the Assessment Handbook to monitor children's progress.

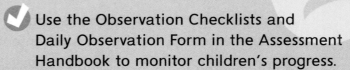

Differentiated Instruction

3-Year-Olds and Extra Support

Objective Listen and retell; practice new vocabulary

Materials Retelling Cards; props, fingerplay puppets, Teacher's Resource Book p. 110

Act It Out Provide props or fingerplay puppets for children to act out the story. See Teacher's Resource Book page 110. Assign children parts. Allow children to retell the story multiple times, switching the child who plays the part of the turtle. Display the Retelling Cards so children can use them to aid in retelling.

Transitional K and Advanced Learners

Objective Listen and retell; practice new vocabulary

Materials Retelling Cards

Retell Place the Retelling Cards on the table. Have children work together to put them in the proper sequence (beginning, middle, end). Then have children retell the story to a partner. They can use the Retelling Cards as reference. Circulate and listen in on the retellings. Prompt children to imagine what instruments other animals might play.

 **English Learners**

Objective Listen and retell; practice new vocabulary

Materials Retelling Cards; pictures

Develop Vocabulary Review the pictures for the story words: *turtle, flute, cage, soup, laughed.* Name each picture, and have children repeat. Say a word. Guide children to find the picture and say the picture name as they pick it up. Then have children name a card for their classmates to find.

Talk About It Display the Retelling Cards, one at a time. Ask children to name items in each picture. Then act out the scene depicted as you state a sentence to summarize what you are doing (e.g., *The turtle hid.*). Have children repeat the actions while saying the sentence.

CiRCLE TiME

WHOLE GROUP

Let's Explore

Objective Learn that heat can change matter; observe motion

Materials popcorn kernels, cooked popcorn, sheet, foam ball

Pop the Popcorn Show children uncooked popcorn. Ask: *How would you describe this popcorn?* (hard, small, yellow). Show some cooked popcorn and ask: *How has the popcorn changed?* (bigger, softer, white) *What do you think made it change?* (heat)

- Tell children they are going to pretend the foam ball is a popcorn kernel and they are going to bounce it on the sheet to make it "pop."

- Have each child hold the edge of the sheet. Place the foam ball in the middle. Encourage children to try to keep the ball in the air by moving the sheet up and down. Discuss how kernels are moved around through hot air in order for them to pop.

- If possible, allow children to watch popcorn pop to see that heat causes the kernels to change. Ask: *How can you describe the sound you hear?*

Teacher Table

4-Year-Olds

Objective Meet next year's teacher

Materials none

Welcome to Kindergarten Take children to visit their next year's kindergarten class.

- Afterward, have them describe what is the same and different.

- Have them "play" kindergarten in the Dramatic Play Center.

- Reinforce all the ways they are ready for next year.

CSP_Garsya/Fotosearch LBRF/age fotostock

Art and Construction Center

Body Art Children continue to create paintings using finger-, thumb-, and handprints.

Focus on Grammar Work with children to use "my" or "mine" to indicate their work, and "his" or "her" to identify the work of others. Model, as needed.

 Use the Observation Checklists and Daily Observation Form in the Assessment Handbook to monitor children's progress.

Differentiated Instruction

3-Year-Olds and Extra Support

Objective Celebrate learning

Materials art supplies, large sheets of construction paper

Celebrate Learning Remind children that they have learned a lot this year. One of the most important things is how to recognize their name.

- Give children art supplies. Have them create their name in any way they choose on a large sheet of construction paper.

- Then have children draw pictures of things they've learned this year.

- Provide time for children to share their pictures. Take a photo of children and tape it on the picture. If you have copies of the photos you took at the beginning of the year, tape it beside the new photo.

Transitional K and Advanced Learners

Objective Meet next year's teacher

Materials none

Welcome to Kindergarten Take children to visit their next year's kindergarten class.

- Afterward, have them describe what is the same and different.

- Have them "play" kindergarten in the Dramatic Play Center.

- Reinforce all the ways they are ready for next year.

- Have children draw and write a note for their next-year's teacher.

Ken Cavanagh/McGraw-Hill Education

EL English Learners

Objective Build theme-related vocabulary

Materials none

Oral Language Have children share some of the fun things they did with you this year. Explain that many of them will be going to kindergarten next year. If possible, introduce them to their next-year's teacher.

CiRCLE TiME

WHOLE GROUP

Objectives Review and assess

Materials Assessment Flip Book

Assessment Flip Book

Day 1

Patterns Review

- Place a set of shape blocks in a bag. Have children grab a shape from the bag and describe it to the class. Confirm identity by revealing the shape. Then place a pile of shapes on the table, multiples of each shape. Call out a shape name for children to find. Have them hold up their shape.

- Use the shape manipulatives to create patterns (e.g., AB, AAB, ABB, and ABA). Have children identify the pattern, then extend it.

Day 2

Counting Review

- Guide children to count as high as they can as you march around the room. Take note of where children "trail off." Review counting to 30.

- Display a set of counters. Ask: *How many do I have?* Have children chorally count, then name the amount. Repeat with amounts from 0–30.

- Say a number, such as 4, and have children count to 10 (or beyond) from your starting point. Repeat with different starting and ending points.

Teacher Table

All Learners

Assessment Select several children to assess each day during Teacher Table time. Administer the tests individually. Record the results and your observations to determine each child's academic growth throughout the year and to inform the child's kindergarten teacher. Use these assessments from the Assessment Flip Book: Counting, Numbers, Shapes, Patterns, Colors, Sorting.

Math and Manipulatives Center

Math Games Children engage with games requiring counting, include games with dice and dominoes.

Mini Motor Counters Children use the counters and cards to review and practice Pre-K math skills.

Numerals Review

- Place the numeral cards on the table in random order. Have children work together to order them.

- Once in order, have children briefly close their eyes. Remove a numeral card. Then have children determine which card is missing

- Display a numeral card (0–10). Have children create a matching set of counters.

Counting Review

- Display a row of three counters or manipulatives, each with a different color or shape. Ask: *Which is first? Second? Third?* Repeat with other rows of counters. Then line up children and have children chorally give the ordinal placement of each child (e.g., Marco is first, Selena is second, and so on).

- Place a small set of counters in your hand. Briefly open your hand. Ask: *How many do I have?* Then close your hand. Record children's responses. Open your hand and chorally count with children to confirm.

Addition and Subtraction Review

- Use counters and simple word problems to guide children to add to 5. Extend based on children's abilities.

- Use counters and simple word problems to guide children to subtract from 5. Extend based on children's abilities.

Go Digital

Each child should complete computer activities individually as you (or an assistant) periodically monitors and guides.

Weekly Data Each week create a different graph to organize data. You might also wish to take an existing graph and display the information in a new way (e.g., change a T-chart into a bar graph). Ask questions about the graph's content and connect the information to mathematical concepts.

Daily Math Talk While children are exploring in the centers, use narrating, revoicing, and asking open-ended questions to develop mathematical understandings and problem-solving skills. Discuss with children the strategies they are using.

Music and Movement

CiRCLE TiME

WHOLE GROUP

Literacy Through Music

Objective Practice left-to-right tracking

Materials Big Book of Nursery Rhymes pp. 16-17,
Teacher's Resource Book p. 115, tapping pieces

Teddy Bear

Teddy bear, teddy bear,
Turn around.

Teddy bear, teddy bear,
Touch the ground.

Teddy bear, teddy bear,
Show your shoe.

Teddy bear, teddy bear,
That will do.

16

17

- Play the recording and review the movements of the song.

- Display the Big Book and invite children to join you singing the song as you point to each word.

- Place the tapping page, Teacher's Resource Book page 115, on a table so all can see.

- Review the small manipulative used to tap the page. Place this tapping piece by the arrow.

- Distribute tapping pages. Have children practice with their fingers before you distribute tapping pieces, then sing as they tap on the page.

Let's Sing

Objective Develop creative movements for a song

Materials audio, scarves or streamers (optional)

Gogo

Kenyan Folk Song

Sung by Mary Okari

English Words by Linda Worsley

1 Your feet turn out! everybody go-go.
  You spin about, everybody go-go.
  Then bend your knees and walk
  down low, everybody go-go.
  And wave your hands and make
  a show, everybody go-go.

2 Walk on your toes, everybody go-go. . . .

3 Walk backwards now, everybody go-go. . . .

Play the recording and invite children to move in place as they listen.

- Explain that this is a singing game from Kenya, Africa, about silly ways of walking. African children traditionally make up funny ways to walk as they sing the song.

- Review the words, pointing out the actions, and guide children to create movements for each verse.

- Divide the class into two groups, one to do the movements as the other group watches and sings along with the recording. Switch roles and repeat.

- Try using one verse as a transition song to move children to a new activity.

Outdoor Play PHYSICAL DEVELOPMENT

Allot at least 30 minutes a day for outdoor play. Create a chart that shows when children can play on specific equipment to teach sharing and turn taking.

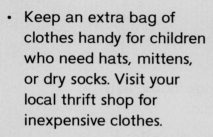

- Keep an extra bag of clothes handy for children who need hats, mittens, or dry socks. Visit your local thrift shop for inexpensive clothes.

- Set up activities and games that require children to hop on one foot, stop and change directions, walk on a balance beam (e.g., masking tape line), jump up, jump forward, and other gross motor movements.

- Provide support and protection when children climb on bars, hang upside down, etc.

Indoor Play FINE MOTOR SKILLS

Morning Movement
- Use "Morning Movement" audio every day to help build children's muscular strength, endurance, and flexibility.

Motor Assessment
- Formally assess children's motor skills using the Motor Assessments in the Assessment Flip Book.

- Use the following assessments: hopping, walking a straight line, throwing a ball, catching a ball, kicking a ball, holding a pencil correctly, drawing lines, writing first name, and cutting a straight line.

Let's Move GROSS MOTOR SKILLS

Objective Develop gross-motor skills; play a strong beat pattern on instruments

Materials audio, dramatic play props, rhythm instruments

Tell children that England's King George II loved music. For a special celebration, he asked his royal composer, George Frederic Handel, to write new music. All the king's family and friends came to hear the concert in a park.

- Play the Rhythm Track recording of "Minuet II," and have children pat their knees with the strong beat.

- Invite children to have a parade around the classroom as they listen to the king's music. Ask: *What would you wear? How would you walk? Would you wave and smile? Would you bow to the king at the end of the parade?*

- Give children rhythm instruments and guide them in playing and moving with the strong beat as they create a regal parade.

Assessment

Performance Assessment

☑ **Observation** Use the *Daily Observation Form,* on Assessment Handbook page 6 throughout the unit.

- Select two to four children each day to observe.

- Make sure all children are observed multiple times throughout the unit.

- Use the observations to form small groups for additional instruction and to record each child's progress on the *Unit 9 Checklist,* on Assessment Handbook pages 23–24.

Formal Assessment

Administer the following assessments from the Assessment Flip Book individually. Record each child's results and place them in their Student Portfolio.

- **Language:** following directions, labeling objects, position words, opposites, rhyme, identifying same/different words, naming upper- and lowercase letters, letter sounds, differentiating numbers and letters, book handling

- **Motor:** hopping; walking a straight line; throwing, catching, and kicking a ball; holding a pencil; drawing and cutting lines; writing first name

- **Math:** counting, comparing and ordering numbers, recognizing numbers and subitizing, numerals, shapes, patterns

Work Samples

PORTFOLIO

Add one or more of the following to each child's portfolio. Date the samples and add your observations and/or comments on self-stick notes. Use the work samples when conferencing with parents or forming small groups for additional instruction. Use the *Portfolio Teacher Form* and *Portfolio Rubric* on Assessment Handbook pages 28–29.

- Writing/Drawing samples from the Writing Center or children's journal entries.

- Sample of child writing his/her name.

Ken Cavanagh/McGraw-Hill Education

Image Source/age fotostock

Developmental Red Flags

Articulation

Watch for the child:

✓ Whose speech is difficult to understand, compared with peers

✓ Who mispronounces sounds

✓ Whose mouth seems abnormal (excessive under- or overbite, swallowing difficulty, poorly lined-up teeth)

✓ Who has difficulty putting words and sounds in proper sequence

✓ Who cannot be encouraged to produce age-appropriate sounds

✓ Who has a history of ear infections or middle ear disorders

NOTE Most children develop the following sounds correctly by the ages shown.

2 years old—all vowel sounds

3 years old—*p, b, m, w, h*

4 years old—*t, d, n, k, g, ng*

5 years old—*f, j, sh*

6 years old—*ch, v, r, l*

7 years old—*s, z, th*

Assessment Tools

Assessment Handbook

Daily Observation Form
Assessment Handbook page 6

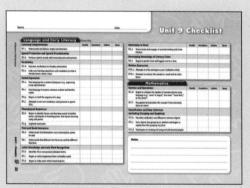

Unit 9 Checklist
Assessment Handbook pages 23–24

Assessment Flip Book

Additional Resources

Outdoor Play

Children need the space and time each day to run, jump, shout, climb, and play together. Outdoor time is a critical part of each instructional day. The benefits of outdoor play include:

- Developing gross motor skills
- Developing healthy bodies
- Learning to play respectfully together
- Learning to resolve conflicts
- Releasing extra energy to help focus on indoor activities

Outdoor Play Preparation

- Allot at least 30 minutes a day.

- Create a chart that shows when children can play on specific equipment to teach sharing and turn taking.

- Provide support and protection when children climb on bars, hang upside down, etc.

- Keep a bag of extra clothes handy for children who need hats, mittens, or dry socks. Visit your local thrift shop for inexpensive clothes.

- Observe children during play and keep anecdotal records. Notice leaders, followers, those who need help developing gross motor skills, and those who need help joining in.

- Keep first-aid supplies handy, such as tissues, bandages, and latex gloves, for those scrapes, runny noses, and other minor mishaps.

- Always have adult supervision. If a child needs to be taken inside, never leave children alone.

Outdoor Games and Activities

- Use "Morning Movement" every day to help build children's muscular strength, endurance, and flexibility.

- Play games such as Duck, Duck, Goose; Freeze Tag; Red Rover, Red Rover; 1-2-3 Red Light; Simon Says; and Mother, May I.

- Have lots of balls, jump ropes, beanbags, and sidewalk chalk handy.

- Make extra balls out of socks tied and filled with rice.

- Read a good book outdoors on a sunny day.

- Teach and encourage jump rope rhymes to build phonological awareness.

- Create an outdoor obstacle course.

- Show how to create a shadow.

- Sing songs that involve a lot of movement.

- Maintain balance when climbing steps.

- Provide bubbles for bubble play.

Sign Language

Twenty signs are taught and used throughout the program
to more effectively manage the classroom environment.

bathroom

come

eat

focus

go

help

listen

look

no

now

play

please

quietly

sit

stop

talk

time

wait

walk

yes

Ken Cavanagh/McGraw-Hill Education

Theme Bibliography

READY FOR KINDERGARTEN

Fiction

Blueberries for Sal
Robert McCloskey (Penguin)
Sal and her mother are picking blueberries along with some unexpected company.

The Greatest Gymnast of All
Stuart J. Murphy, Cynthia Jabar (illustrator) (HarperCollins)
As Zoe shows off her gymnastic abilities, she also illustrates opposites such as in and out, and up and down.

Hilda Must Be Dancing
Karma Wilson, Suzanne Watts (illustrator) (Children's Book Press)
Hilda the Hippo loves dancing, even if everyone around her has trouble with her form of self-expression.

Kindergarten Countdown
Anna Jane Hays, Linda Davick (illustrator)
A girl counts down the days to school by describing what she'll do in kindergarten.

Kindergarten Rocks!
Katie Davis
(HMH Books for Young Readers)
A boy and his stuffed dog prepare for kindergarten.

The Kissing Hand
Audrey Penn, Ruth E. Harper and Nancy M. Leak (illustrators)
This heartwarming classic deals with separation of a child from his/her parents.

The Listening Walk
Paul Showers, Aliki (illustrator) (Harper Trophy)
A father and daughter take a walk and listen to the sounds around them.

Max
Rachel Isadora
(Simon and Schuster)
Max is a baseball player who learns that ballet is a great way to warm up for a home run.

Wemberly Worried
Kevin Henkes
Worried Wemberly realizes that school is too much fun to be worried about.

Nonfiction

The Busy Body Book
Lizzy Rockwell (Alfred A. Knopf)
Children learn about the amazing machine called the "body" and how it works when we're on the move.

A Cool Drink of Water
Barbara Kerley
(National Geographic)
This book discusses how water is basic to human life and well-being.

Eating Right
Mary Elizabeth Salzmann
(SandCastle)
This book explains the value of eating the right foods in the right amounts for proper nutrition.

Five Senses
Margaret Miller
(Children's Book Press)
Five children talk about their senses.

Hands Can
Cheryl Willis Hudson, John Francis-Bourke (illustrator) (Candlewick Press)
Color photographs illustrate some fine- and gross-motor activities that involve hands.

I Can Play Soccer
Edana Eckert
(Children's Book Press)
This book of easy-to-read text and photographs shows Carlos playing soccer with other children.

This Is the Way We Go to School
Edith Baer, Steve Bjorkman (illustrator)
Reader learn how children around the world go to school.

ABC Books

Animal Action ABC
Karen Pandell, Nancy Sheehan (illustrator) (Dutton)
Children imitate animals as they move and stretch through the ABCs.

Food ABC
Patricia Whitehouse
(Heinemann)
Each letter of the alphabet is illustrated with a popular food.

LMNO Peas
Keith Baker
Cute peas with a wide array of occupations and interests introduce the alphabet.

Museum ABC
The New York Metropolitan Museum of Art
Children are introduced to great works of art as they learn the alphabet.

Index

Vv

Ww